3 1403 000

W9-CCH-361

137.7
KUR

Kurdsen
Graphology.

DATE DUE

6 Jul '84			
FEB 0 4 '86			
NOV 07 '87			
DEC 12 '87			
MAY 15 '88			
SEP 06 '88			
FEB 0 2 '92			
MAR 31 '92			
APR 21 '92			
MAY 1 2 '92			
MAY 0 6 '93			

GAYLORD   PRINTED IN U.S.A.

Graphology
The new Science

Graphology
The new Science

Stephen Kurdsen
Foreword by
Jeane Dixon

Galahad Books • New York

© STEPHEN KURDSEN 1971

All rights reserved. No part of this publication
may be reproduced, stored in retrieval system,
or transmitted, in any form or by any means,
electronic, mechanical, photocopying, recording
or otherwise, without the prior permission
of David & Charles (Publishers) Limited

Library of Congress Catalog Card Number: 73-88100
ISBN 0-88365-234-X

Published by arrangement with Acropolis Books Ltd.

All inquiries should be addressed to
Acropolis Books Ltd, 2400 17th St, N.W., Washington, D.C. 200

Printed in the United States of America

Foreword

'Graphology, the new Science' is a scholarly and comprehensive volume, both useful and practical for professional and business people as well as for fun and self-knowledge.

Written in simple yet concise language, generously illustrated, this book answers many of the most common questions people ask about themselves, their traits and characteristics.

It will give the key to many personality problems and act as a handy reference work on handwriting analysis for those interested in graphology.

Long ago reputable scientists admitted the unmistakable relationship between one's handwriting and one's character . . . and of all so-called 'fortune-telling methods', handwriting indentification is still the only one accepted as evidence in a court of law.

Summing up his years of study on the subject, Mr Stephen Kurdsen shares with you in this book the fundamentals of his years of study, and his exceptional grasp and knowledge of the complex and fascinating science of graphology.

Jeane Dixon

Contents

Introduction

Graphology: its value and limitations

WE are all born with a deep need to communicate—to share our thoughts, our feelings, our experiences with others. The way we speak, the way we dress, even our most subtle changes of facial expression are all a means of telling the world who and what we are.

Of course, many of us have thoughts and emotions which we wish to keep secret from our fellow men. But to the trained observer even these hidden feelings are uncovered by certain signs. The psychiatrist senses the undercurrents in a person's make-up and is usually adept in spotting small clues which enable him to evaluate the patient on a level not revealed on the surface. But no psychologist is infallible in his own particular method of uncovering traits of character and personality. A second professional opinion is often valuable.

The bright, cheerful man or woman who radiates charm and good humour may sometimes be hiding morbid or destructive thoughts. An obviously disturbed person may have unsuspected drives and resources for mental health. Only time and thorough and expert testing will uncover the hidden traits. One test which many psychologists consider a useful clinical tool—rather than a parlour game—is a handwriting evaluation by an expert graphologist.

Graphology has one advantage over other tests: it yields a vivid picture of the subject without him being present in the flesh or without him being asked to speak a single word. Like all approaches to human understanding, it has had to battle for recognition. The fact that today it has become an increasingly acceptable part of the armoury of the psychiatrist, the doctor, the personnel officer, the insurance investigator, is due to the diligence and enthusiasm of the pioneers in the science.

It is becoming recognised that our tendency to clap neat little labels on the people we know needs counteraction. We say that Jim is selfish; Mary is a bore; Hugh is a pseudo-intellectual; Jane is an empty-headed prattler; Margaret is anti-social and a prig with a smirk on her face; Bernard is peculiar. But this is the most superficial judgment and we are not digging deep enough. If you are a personnel selection consultant your hasty summing up of a job applicant's character by physical appearance and mannerisms may be sadly out of joint.

To gain a true picture of Jim, Mary, Hugh and the rest, their handwriting will help. You can take a closer look at yourself, too, through your own handwriting. Of course, you will have to estimate very carefully, balance each positive feature against each negative one, each strength against each weakness. You will discover traits and talents you never suspected existed in people you thought you knew well. And by means of your own handwriting you will discover potentials within yourself of which you were hitherto unaware, or personality traits which you may wish to eliminate or perhaps to strengthen.

No two handwritings are exactly alike, just as no two people are exactly alike. A study of graphology may force you gradually to drop your old labels and reevaluate your friends, your associates, your employees. As your knowledge grows, you will gain more and more insight into what makes people tick. You can select your friends from people you discover to have common interests and common emotional traits. You can learn how to judge compatibility in marriage, how to be more understanding with your friends and relations. You will be better able to judge that new man you were thinking of hiring or that boss you were thinking of joining.

Graphology tells us a great deal about the make-up of a person, but there are two things it does not reveal. No graphological analysis will reveal with absolute certainty the sex of the writer. In all of us there are both masculine and feminine components which often have nothing to do with physiology. The extreme cases are the men whom we consider effeminate or the women whose manner and dress cause them to be regarded as masculine. In analysing handwriting we are therefore somewhat in the dark on that score. Thus it is important to learn by some other means the sex of the writer rather than to guess. Even the expert could be mistaken.

Handwriting does not show a person's age either. What it does reveal are signs of maturity—or lack of it. We all know people of mature years who have not grown up emotionally. The hard-boiled business executive who makes practical and astute decisions which affect large sums of money may, when his emotions become involved, act like a little boy. A youth of fifteen may possess more poise and sense of responsibility than a man of forty-five who drinks and gambles his money away.

Old age will usually be revealed in handwriting that is tremulous with wavering strokes. But it does not follow that the aged are the only people who write such a hand. A person under great tension or a chronic drinker might also do so. Then again, there are many old people whose handwriting shows steadiness, animation and enthusiasm. Thus it is important that we know the chronological age of the writer before we prepare our analysis.

There are many things which spring to mind as obstacles to clear, concise analysis of handwriting. The regrettable effects of the near-universal use of the ball point pen, the minor variations to which many people's writing is subject daily, the use of the left instead of the more usual right hand may, on the surface, appear to affect the analysis. But the use of a ball point pen affects only the pen pressure—it cannot affect the margins, the slant, the size of the writing, the space between lines, words and letters, the direction of the lines, nor indeed the construction of each individual letter.

Depression, worry, optimism, happiness—all these moods can alter slightly the appearance of a writing, but these are only temporary moods and indeed the overall concept shows them to be temporary, as will be seen later in the book. Left-handedness may or may not be a psychological symptom or a psychological cause but, to date, statistics have proved little, and we find people of all personality categories among the left-handed.

An expert can make a tentative analysis from a word or a signature—but he seldom does. He knows he is treading on thin ice, and that the characteristic which may appear in that one word may not appear again in two whole pages of writing. Then again, the signature often differs immensely from the body matter in a letter, for the signature is the 'face' we put on for the world and, like a pose, does not reveal the real person. The ideal sample is two pages of writing or one whole page at the very least. It must be on unlined paper and written with the writer's usual pen. Be cautious and exercise extreme care in making an analysis. One characteristic in a page is a tendency; repeated it is a trait.

Chapter 1

Symmetry—The first step

FOR graphological purposes handwriting is divided into three zones. The zone doctrine was first formulated by Pulver in 1930. By many tests and experiments he was able to discard the intuitive side of handwriting analysis which had been prevalent for more than two hundred years and develop graphology into a real science. His zone doctrine has never been successfully challenged, and has widened and clarified the use of the science to a remarkable degree.

With his three zones method it is fairly obvious that Pulver took up and adapted for graphology the personality structure concepts of Freud: the Super-Ego, the Ego, the Id. The following diagram illustrates the Freudian theory as applied by the graphologist:

1
UPPER ZONE   *flight*   intellect/ethics/imagination
MIDDLE ZONE   daily routine/habits
LOWER ZONE   instinct/urges/intuition

THE UPPER ZONE is that which takes in the loops of the letters **b, l, h**, etc. It is located in the conscious. There we have ethics, intellect, imagination, ideas.

THE MIDDLE ZONE takes in the small letters like **a, e, o, c**, etc. It deals with the daily routine—habits, customs, likes and dislikes, social relations.

THE LOWER ZONE takes in the loops of the letters **y, g, z,** etc. It is located in the unconscious. There we have emotions, instincts, intuition, drives, urges.

We see that the upper loops reveal a man's dream life, his ideals, his fantasies. Other high strokes corroborate his reaching up. If the purely physical or sexual demands made on him by his own instinctive nature are stronger than he can cope with in the normal course of daily living, he may be a person whose intellect and emotions are in conflict. Or he may effect a compromise between his ideals and primitive demands so that he can function with some serenity on the realistic plane. If he achieves such a compromise we refer to him as well-adjusted, and we see a similarity of size in the lower and upper loops.

If, on the other hand, his instinctual drives are very strong, we see an over-strong loop in the lower zone, reaching to a good length. We can judge the balance between intellect and instinct from these upper and lower loops. So we see that, if the upper, lower and middle zones are uniform (2) it indicates an even, peaceable temperament with a love of method and order, contemplative and serene. Because the writer has his intellectual and his instinctual feelings or drives under control, he may also be rather rigid, callous, unresponsive—sometimes apathetic.

Sometimes we meet a handwriting in which there is little uniformity. The upper loops are sometimes tall, sometimes short. The lower loops reach right down or stretch for very little distance (3). A method of dealing with the upper and lower loops such as this indicates a certain impressionability and sensitivity. It also points to curiosity, alertness, excitability. There is irritability and moodiness here, a critical nature, and perhaps a touch of crankiness.

The upper zone may be over-developed and 'reach for the sky', (4) and this denotes enthusiasm, idealism, pride, a feeling for religion. There is ambition, too, but as there is too much emphasis on the upper zone with not enough on the realistic or instinctual zones, there will

2 *the ugly duckling*

3 *a gruff-voiced fellow*

4 *Pride before a fall*

5 **lack of ideas**

be the lack of ability to achieve that ambition. Nevertheless the writer is probably conceited, though with a lack of objectivity. He may be egocentric and a little irritable, and though he is zealous, his frustrated ambition tends to make him a little unruly.

Pity the writer who neglects the upper zone and leaves the loops of the **h, b, l,** etc short. There is no conceit—but then there is nothing to be conceited about. His tendency to waste no space on the upper zone (5) shows that he is materialistic, not very bright. In fact his intellect and his power of creating ideas will be sadly lacking. And because of his lack of imagination coupled with ideals, he may also be lacking in any religious feeling.

Some people place emphasis on the middle zone to the detriment of the upper and lower (6). They will appear self-assured, even presumptuous, and their over-compensated inferiority complex looks very much like conceit. This exaggeration of the middle zone also indicates sentimentality, femininity, an over-concern with self.

6 *SENTIMENTALITY*

7 *Philosophy*

8 *matter of fact*

9 *money bags*

The middle zone may be neglected (7), which indicates that the writer is rather reserved, frugal and modest. He has a sense of objectivity and a philosophical outlook. Though he is masculine in his make-up, he nevertheless has an inferiority complex. And he is rather impractical.

The lower zone—that which deals with the instinctual drives—may be overdeveloped with pressure (8) and this indicates a healthy, physical appetite, including sexual impulses, heaviness, sentimentality, matter-of-factness. The writer will be realistic, of athletic tendency, and with technical talent. Slow-thinking, he will be conscientious and will pay great attention to detail. He will be rather sober in outlook.

The lower loops may be long, but without pressure (9). There is a money complex here, a search for security, financial or otherwise. Indeed, many graphologists and psychologists have referred to the long, weak lower loops as 'money bags'.

Sometimes one sees right-slanting or upright writing with the lower zone loops slanting left against all the rules. The loops may be heavy. If they are, it indicates opposition to or frustration in sexual intercourse. With no pressure, in the presence of pressure in left-right strokes, it indicates heavy lapses of potency (10).

At the opposite end of the scale, the lower zone may be sadly neglected, with very short loops to the letters y, g, etc (11). Here we have a writer who shows a certain lack of realistic outlook, a lack of sense for material necessities. There will probably be sexual immaturity, sexual fear or trauma. Doctors have also found this writing trait in the script of patients with damaged or incapacitated legs or feet.

There appears to be no such thing as a well-developed single zone. If one zone is clearly more strongly developed than the other two, it is usually over-

B

developed. And over-development of one zone always occurs at the expense of one or both of the others.

Absolute symmetry in handwriting **(12)** exists only in theory. We accept a script as symmetrical if the letters of each zone are more or less of the same height, width and slant, and the proportions of the letters harmonious. The 'more or less' standard is the one which we have to accept. Anything better—absolutely perfect symmetry— would be of purely mechanical or artificial origin. The writer of a good symmetrical hand is probably not a very lively or imaginative person. He is reliable, helpful, industrious, the good citizen who will not really enrich our lives with any demonstration of genius.

SUMMARY

General uniformity
Even and peaceable in temperament; contemplative; fond of order; serene; indifferent; rigid; callous; apathetic

No uniformity
Impressionable; sensitive; curious; alert; moody; irritable; critical; excitable; cranky.

Upper zone over-developed
Enthusiastic; idealistic; religious; proud; ambitious but lacking in ability to realise it; lacking in objectivity; eccentric; irritable; conceited; zealous.

Upper zone neglected
Irreligious; non-intellectual; lacking in imagination and ideas; materialistic.

Middle zone over-developed
Sentimental; feminine; over-concerned with self; self-assured; conceited (over-compensated inferiority complex).

Middle zone neglected
Reserved; objective; philosophical in outlook; modest; masculine; impractical; has inferiority complex.

Lower zone over-developed
Heavy; sentimental; matter-of-fact; realistic; athletic; talented in a technical way; conscientious; sober; attentive to detail; slow-thinking.

Lower zone neglected
Lacking a realistic outlook; lacking a sense for material necessities; sexually immature; possessing a sexual fear or trauma.

Long lower loops without pressure
Possessing a money complex; searching for security.

Left-slanting heavy lower loop in right-slanting writing
An opposition to or frustration in sexual intercourse.

Same stroke with no pressure where there is pressure in left-right strokes
Heavy lapses of potency

Pen pressure

When considering pen pressure it is also important to consider the type of pen a person chooses, because the analyst can then deduce more from the type of pen pressure he employs. He may be using a pen entirely unsuited to his type of pressure.

A person who prefers a stub pen may even go through the paper when he writes with a fine point. The choice of a stub pen already tells us that his pressure is heavy or medium-heavy so we know he belongs in the fundamental or materialistic category. When we say that a person who writes with heavy pressure is generally materialistic, the word does not necessarily imply that he is grasping or money-mad. His interest is mainly in concrete reality, in things he can see, hear, feel and taste. But every handwriting will have corroborating signs which will tell you whether the person under scrutiny is essentially materialistic or only just partly so.

In writing one has to press the ink-filled pen against the paper and at the same time the fingers must be pressed around the pen holder. The pressure against the paper indicates our display of vigour, strength and vitality. The pressure on the pen-holder reveals the aims and the inner convictions behind that display. Under heavy pen-paper pressure the pen traces a heavy, thick line over the paper; with slight pressure, the line remains fine and light.

Generally, down strokes are heavy, up strokes light.

Curved lines are partly heavy and partly light. Pen-paper pressure can therefore be quite accurately appraised through observing the contrast between the thinner up strokes and the heavier down strokes. With normal pens, where there is no contrast there is no pen-paper pressure no matter how heavy the writing appears in general.

If you suspect pressure without on the face of it definite proof, the reverse side of the paper will actually show the degree of pen-paper pressure. When we examine writing, our fingers should glide over the furrows on the reverse side of the paper because we can feel pen-paper pressure which the eye may not detect.

Pressure on the pen-holder cannot be recognised easily but some clues can be drawn from the appearance of the writing. Very small and neat characters, particularly angles, suggest that the type of pressure used was similar to that of the characters—neat and firm. The constant regular change between light and heavy strokes cannot be carried out without a tightly gripped pen.

It is only with due consideration of a hand's pen-holder pressure that we can arrive at any conclusive interpretation of pen-paper pressure. Strong pen-paper pressure in the down strokes together with evident pen-holder pressure may indicate a strongly disciplined will and a readiness to fight for one's ideals. But without the pen-holder pressure there may be bellicosity and a claim to leadership which may border on dictatorship.

The heavy-pressure writer (13) is usually physically robust. He is for the most part the outdoor individual interested in athletics. He may be a businessman primarily interested in the material results of his efforts. There is a strong element of the primitive in him and he has healthy physical appetites. He is probably an adventurer by instinct, and is often intensely emotional, impulsive, concerned much more with activity than in spending time in contemplation. He is a doer, often a pioneer. He probably enjoys working with his hands. If there is pressure on the down strokes and none elsewhere, he may have an over-compensated sexual insufficiency, sexual inhibition. He may be over-ambitious, irritable, egocentric with a certain cockiness.

The medium-pressure writing (14) is found in the letters of people in every walk of life. For this type of writer the interest is often divided between people and things. It is the normal type of pressure and by itself gives no clue to the personality or character of the writer.

The person who chooses a pen with a fine point already tells us that he is rather sensitive (15). His approach to life is not heavy-footed and he has spirituality, refinement, quiet tastes and manners. He is modest, simple, unassuming, has a certain mobility, alertness and adaptability. There is ability here, together

13 *This is heavy*

14 *This is medium*

15 *This is fine or very fine*

16 *Shaded writing.*

17 *Now is the time for all good*

18 *Copybook Style*

with optimism. Because he is sensitive and has delicacy of feeling, he is also on the feminine side but there may be irritability, a lack of substantiality, a lack of inhibition. The light pressure writing which is also over-large indicates a lack of discipline, in some cases even lawlessness.

Should the writing be very fine the qualities of quiet taste and manners, of spirituality, of modesty are more pronounced. There is shyness, a lack of energy. The writer is not aggressive, is kind, tender, and never tries to dominate others.

Some writers tend to 'shade' their writing (16). The up strokes are thin and the down strokes thick in a uniform manner. If they are shaded just a little it indicates an insistent nature, a distinctive personality.

When we speak of pressure and its absence we always assume a pressure pattern that appears harmoniously in down strokes of the writing. But certain persons cannot or will not follow the natural rhythm. Their pressure comes in strange and threatening lumps (17). This phenomenon has been noticed quite often in the handwriting of criminals with homicidal tendencies. There are many dark spots and heavy strokes in this type of script, but they are not arranged to any reasonable, natural order. At the least the writer will probably be found to be a hypocrite, deceitful and dishonest. He definitely will not be a man to be trusted. Indeed, he is to be avoided, especially in a business deal.

Some people, having been taught at school the beautiful copybook style (18), have made no effort to alter it by initiative or any creative talent and the mere fact that they stick so closely to the writing they have been taught stamps them as over-conventional and with little ambition. They will be sticklers for conventional forms and fads, never take creative risks, and possess purely commonplace personalities.

THE WRITER AND THE INK

The most generally used colour in ink is dark blue, or blue-black but there are people who prefer vividly coloured inks—red or green. They are the same people who like vividly coloured blouses, ties and wallpaper. They usually have highly-developed senses.

Although ink is a liquid, most people can write with it and yet produce a clean script; others cannot **(19)**, and like their writing, their thoughts, actions or bodies are

19 *this — is not clean*

20 *The ink flows down*

not very clean either. They are not to be confused with those very sensuous people whose ink has a tendency to flow, as it were, more freely, and then to escape. In some cases the tendency is for the ink to flow towards the lower zone **(20)**, which is interpreted as an indication of an oversexed temperament.

SUMMARY

Very fine
Lacking energy; quiet; modest; non-aggressive; shy; kind; tender; not wishing to dominate others.

Fine
Spiritual; refined; with quiet tastes and manners; modest; simple.

Medium-heavy
Means nothing by itself.

Average, shaded a little
Possessing an insistent nature; a distinctive personality.

Heavy
Materialistic; sensuous; strong willed; persevering; diligent; resolute; severe; self-confident; possessing a love of eating and other physical pleasures; possessing love of outdoor sports in which skill and athleticism count.

Smeary, pasty writing, uneven pressure; some letters thin, others thick
Hypocritical; deceitful; dishonest.

Ink appears to flow to lower zone
Over-sexed temperamentally.

Copybook style
Over-conventional; possessing little ambition; purely commonplace.

Pressure on down strokes, none elsewhere
Possessing an over-compensated sexual insufficiency; sexually inhibited; over-ambitious; cocky; irritable; ego-centric.

Fine script, over-large
Lacking in discipline; lawless.

Chapter 2

The margins

THE margin, that area of space to the left, to the right, at the top and at the base of a letter, has a special graphological significance. Many writers will admit some deliberation in the choice of a left margin, but only in exceptional cases is the right margin developed with similar deliberate care. We assume that the left margin is the 'face' that writers insist on showing to a certain extent. The right margin, which is the writer's goal when he starts to write a line, betrays the distance which he really maintains between the world and himself.

A few writers deliberately choose, point by point and line by line, a straight left margin but others are carried away by their enthusiasm, their impatience, and they move the starting point of the written lines more and more to the right (21). In other words, the left margin widens. Other writers cannot entirely fight off their prudence, shyness or innate sense of economy, and therefore with every line move the starting point further and further back to the left (22). The left margin grows narrower. In both these cases the writer's real personality overcomes his intention to show a 'face'.

Wide left margins (23) may be interpreted as an indication of the writer's respect or reservation towards others. They are found in the writings of shy or proud people.

The better-off among us—and those who want to be

taken for such—also often display these wide left margins. If the margins are at the same time very regular, suspicion of a certain anxiety of neurotic or snobbish origin cannot be dismissed.

Only the pathologically self-conscious person will watch and control not only his left margin but the right,

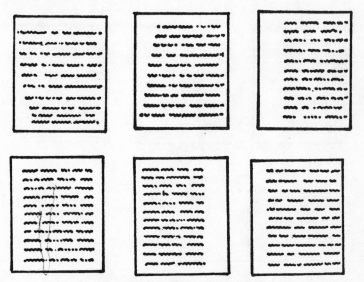

21–26 reading from left to right

too **(24)**. Usually, right margins, unlike the left, are quite ordinarily irregular. Wide right margins indicate a certain withdrawal, a reserve or fear of the future. There is also over-sensitivity, impressionableness or neurosis with the desire to keep the world at a safe distance. Writers who use wide right margins **(25)** are bad mixers who tend to keep the world at a distance. On the other hand, narrow right margins show a certain gregariousness **(26)**. There is vitality, the courage to face life, a predilection for mixing with others, loquacity, perhaps a tendency to act hastily.

Like the left margin, the right may widen towards the bottom of the page too, but the indications are different. Here there is shyness, suspicion, a fear of fellow men **(27)**.

Irregular right margins **(28)** show a certain lack of sense of economy and tell of unwise thrift, but there is also a love of adventure and travel, reserve alternating

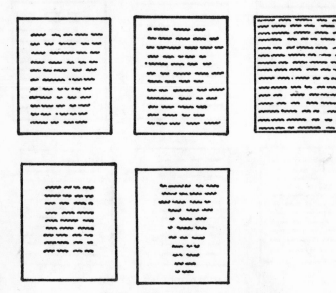

27–31 reading from left to right

with loquacity, gregariousness alternating with a desire to remain alone, and ambivalent social attitudes.

Graphologists have not yet fully explored the interpretation of the upper margin—perhaps because they maintain that it is mainly determined by the size of the letterhead and the address. But on the second sheet of a letter the graphologist has more basis on which to work. We assume that the narrow upper margins reveal informality, and wide ones indicate withdrawal and modesty.

How wide a lower margin we leave indicates how much we concern ourselves with the emotional, sentimental, sexual and material. It can be taken as the lower zone of a letter. A narrow lower margin has been found to be the characteristic of dreamers who let themselves go. If there is pressure in the script, they are probably sensuous. In all events, they are materialistic. A wide lower margin indicates aloofness, idealism, superficiality. It may also mean sexual fear or trauma.

There are letters without margins (29) which indicates that the writer is so economical that it amounts to compulsiveness. He may spend his energy and time lavishly, walking miles to save very little on a purchase. He usually has something put away for a rainy day, and he is obsessed by money because of a fear of the future, even though he may be more than comfortable as regards finance.

Then there is the aesthete or the withdrawn person who writes his letter with wide margins all round (30). The margins are deliberate walls against intruders. Wide margins all round have also been found in the letters of people with phobias and fears. There is a voluntary isolation indicated, with little disposition to join or mix, secrecy about the writer's own affairs, and a delicate taste and sense of beauty and colour.

One indication of the writer's bad management is the urge to fill up the margins with last minute snippets of news. They are as untidy as the PS and the PPS at the end of a letter.

To the sensitive mind the text of a message may have an influence—slight though it be—upon the handwriting and upon the margins. The intelligent and sensitive writer probably cannot avoid being affected by the message where the insensitive dullard puts any message on paper without thought or fear. The margins of the sensitive person may tend to express his position to the person to whom the letter is written, or the mood in which it was written. It is therefore advisable, where the writer is both intelligent and sensitive—proved by other handwriting traits—to examine several letters written at different times before making a rigid analysis.

On very rare occasions one comes across an oddity in the pattern of margins. One such was a letter found a few years ago. On it the left margin, having started as excessively wide, grew smaller, while at the same time the right margin also diminished (31). These painfully contradictory margins were written by a man who suffered from a marked hysterical conflict between fear of people and inability to remain alone.

SUMMARY

Upper margin
Wide: Formal; reserved; modest; withdrawn.
Narrow: Informal; possessing direct approach; lacking in proper respect.

Lower margin
Wide: Superficial; aloof; possessing sexual or emotional fear or trauma.
Narrow: Apt to dream; inclined to mysticism; sentimental. With pressure in script: sensual; materialistic.

Left margin
Wide: Self-respecting; generous; possessing good cultural background and a consciousness of own values; reserved; shy.
Wider: Possessing a fondness for the best in art, music and literature; fond of colour and colour combinations; artistic and somewhat impractical; fussy about small things; self-conscious.
Too wide: Possessing a pretence to or having a cari-

cature of self-respect; generous; shy (sometimes pathologically so).

Narrow: Familiar; free and easy; having a desire for popularity; thrifty; lacking in sense of beauty.

Widening: Hasty; impatient; enthusiastic; oblivious to economic necessities; innately lavish.

Narrowing: Cautious; prudent; shy; suspicious; fearful of fellow men; innately economic.

Right margin
Wide: Reserved; fearful of future; over-sensitive; unable to mix.

Narrow: Having vitality and courage to face life; hasty; good mixer.

Widening: Shy; suspicious; fearful of fellow men.

Irregular: Lacking a sense of economy; practising unwise thrift; possessing reserve alternating with loquacity.

All-round-wide margins
Voluntarily isolated; aloof; spiritually independent; philosophical; secretive about own affairs; possessing delicate taste and sense of beauty and colour; having conviction of own values; having little disposition to join or mix.

No margins
Compulsively economical on food and money; fearful of the future financially.

Direction of the lines

When we first receive instruction in writing, our teacher insists on straight lines—parallel to the upper and lower edges of the paper. We are given lined paper to assist us in maintaining those straight lines. Later we usually discard the help of those lines and rely on our own senses and inclinations but it takes quite an amount of equanimity and self-discipline continuously to think, write and maintain a straight line on a sheet of unlined paper. Deviations from the line must be fairly frequent.

A tired hand and arm quite naturally retire slowly towards the body of the writer, causing the writing to slope downwards (32), but, for the normal person,

32 *now is the time for all*

33 *now is the time for all.*

34 *is the time for all good*

35 *is the time for all*

writing is no difficult task. Some experienced writers can wield a pen for hours on end without tiring. There must be other causes for those descending lines. When the first lines in a letter descend, the writer is probably downcast rather than tired. If he were tired physically he would not start—or finish—the letter.

Descending lines are, generally speaking, interpreted as being caused by pessimism and depression. The concept of this almost wholly psychological cause for the direction of the lines is supported by tests. The depression may be only temporary; the pessimism may be basic. Either way the question of which to apply to a certain writer can be reliably answered by other features in the writing.

A person with right-slanted writing will be less self-conscious and secretive about his moods than a writer with an upright or left-slanted writing (as will be seen later). By the same token, if a person who can produce a straight line permits his moods to show up in his writing, we must stamp him as demonstrative, over-sensitive, self-indulgent, and generally weak as well as moody.

As we have said, it takes quite an amount of self-discipline to maintain a straight line (33). We have discarded the visual aid of the lines ruled on the paper, so we must assume that the comparatively straight line indicates composure, love of method and order, steadfastness. Because the writer refuses to be upset by moods, we may take it that he may be a little dull—always providing, of course, that other features in the writing support that assumption.

Most writers follow with the hand the forward-moving fingers which hold the pen but there are a few who appear to keep the hand firmly rooted in one spot. The line of writing is straight for just so far—then at the end it curves downwards (34). Such partly-curved lines have been seen in the handwriting of people with considerable manual skill.

Optimism is probably the temporary cause of lines which slope upwards (35). If the writing slope continues in that vein for many pages we look for the permanent cause, and find that the writer has ambition, a restless, aggressive, pushing and buoyant spirit. He is probably a cheerful, hopeful person who prefers, no matter what happens, to look upon the bright side. When we think of ambition we think of him aiming up, unlike the descending-line writer whose depression causes him to lose sight of his goal.

Quite often we see arched or convex lines (36). Obviously the writer of these lines has approached his

c

aim with ambition and a pushing spirit, but in a short time his zeal declines and he loses interest and gives up before the task is completed. His mental stamina is such that he cannot be relied upon to forge steadily towards his goal.

Take, on the other hand, the writer of concave lines (37). Here is someone who approaches his task with little optimism. But once he has overcome his initial lack of self-confidence, his zeal increases and he eventually reaches his goal. The cautious person whose goals are high and who wants to explore them fully before undertaking to achieve them usually shows this form of line-direction.

Sometimes the writer causes his words to rise (38). The lines are broken into ascending steps, and the

36 *is the time for all good*

37 *is the time for all*

38 *the time for all good*

39 *is the time for all good*

writer shows over-optimism with not enough stamina. He has constantly to recall himself to reality.

On the other hand we have the words falling like descending steps (39). Here the writer is fighting against moods of depression and an inner resistance to writing in general which he overcomes only to be defeated again.

Occasionally we come across constantly shifting line

directions in a letter **(40)**. We see that the writer is moody and probably has unsteady working habits. The signs sometimes appear in the hand of someone who perhaps has suffered the loss of a loved one, and is living in a confused state of optimism, resignation and

40   *at the Alhambra?*
        to see it the other
        took Mary as well.

        get a chance do not

41   *letters pop up and down*

pessimism, an ambivalence of hopes and fears. This, of course, is purely temporary. If it is permanent it indicates a conflict between reality and hallucination—sometimes amounting to schizophrenia.

Sometimes even the letters seem to stray—they bob up and down upon a stable line **(41)**. Should this be so, the writer will be found to be careless about small things, hardly ever on time for appointments, not altogether reliable in small matters, yet honest and sincere.

A good way to examine the direction of lines is to look at the handwriting from one of its margins by raising the sample almost to the level of the eyes. We can then see even that very small tendency to descent that has been found to be characteristic of writers who have not fully overcome an inferiority complex.

SUMMARY

Straight lines
Composed; believing in method and order; steadfast.

Descending lines
Weak-willed; over-sensitive; self-indulgent; worried or depressed.

Ascending lines
Possessing pushing, buoyant spirit; ambitious; optimistic; restless.

Descending steps
Fighting against depressive moods and inner resistance to writing.

Ascending steps
Over-optimistic with little stamina; having to recall himself to reality.

Arched lines
Ambitious and self-confident but having too little stamina; losing interest before aim is reached.

Hollow lines
Initially pessimistic but growing ambitious and hardworking until aim is reached.

Irregular changes in direction
Unsteady in working habits; possessing mixture of hopes and fears caused by grievous loss. If permanent, in a dilemma between reality and hallucination.

Letters bobbing up and down

Careless about small things; not altogether reliable in small matters, yet honest and sincere; hardly ever on time for appointments.

Chapter 3

Space between lines

THE mature person usually strives for order and understanding. One of the ways in which he does so in handwriting is the distribution of space between the lines. Tests conducted in darkened rooms have proved that the space between the lines is, unlike the space between words, probably deliberately planned.

That is important, for the space between the lines has been recognised as a picture of the writer's mind dependent upon his temporary state. Overlapping lines have been proved to be a sign of mental disorder and, according to Pulver, extremely wide spacing has sometimes been found in the hands of people who have a premonition of impending insanity. Of course, these samples are rare and the spacing is so exaggerated that it can be recognised at first glance. Personnel selection consultants who deal with applications from the executive type seldom report receiving letters carrying this trait. On the other hand, doctors and psychiatrists come across the characteristic on a number of occasions.

Moderately wide spaces between lines must impress us as an example of order and system **(42)**. The writer has an analytical mind which usually stands on hard facts. With his capacity for clear presentation of complicated data, he makes a good executive. He appreciates good manners; indeed, he has good manners himself, and is clean and considerate. There is a lack of

42 *The mature person usually*
for order and understanding.
Of the ways in which he
in handwriting is the

spontaneity in him and this in itself puts him down as a
good organiser.

On occasion we see spacing which is too wide (43)
which makes us revise our favourable first impression
and recognise the pedant or the person who keeps at a
safe distance from us in order better to maintain his

43 *This man wants to keep*

a safe distance from us

to maintain his preferred

preferred blasé attitude. He is possibly very much afraid
of making logical mistakes, is incoherent and perhaps
feeble-minded.

The writer who places small spaces between his lines
(44) tells us that he is the spontaneous type. Here there
may be a real lack of reserve, perhaps even some
muddleheadedness.

Too narrow spaces stress the muddled thinking to an
alarming degree. To the sane, reasonable person it seems
almost unbelievable that some people should have real
difficulty in keeping their written lines apart, but it is a

fact that a mentally-disturbed person, try as he may, cannot always keep his lines apart, and overlaps them in the process. Overlapping lines are an unmistakable warning to the graphologist **(45)**.

The fact that spaces between lines are not hidden but remain open to view and obvious to everyone seems to suggest that some observation should be kept on writing

44　*This is the*
type of man
Small spacees
his linas. He

45　*Overlapping lines cannot*
be avoided by the mentally
distturb. person try as much
as he will he has real
difficulty in keeping his lines
apart and his writing is a
warning to the graphologist
They appear like this.

in schools and colleges. As these spaces represent the picture of the organisation of the writer's mind, that observation should be valuable to those who favour early treatment of mental disorders. The promise of habitual muddleheadedness in office workers which one comes across occasionally would show, too, in the hand-writing.

In some writing, the lower zone descends into the following line's upper zone **(46)**, which indicates that the

46 *This man suffers from a lack of inhibition and an inability to control his*

writer suffers from a lack of inhibitions, inability to control his sexual impulses. In all probability he is over-concerned with instinctual life.

The upper zone may reach into the preceding line's lower zone (47)—an indication of erotic fancies or dreams which are, however, not acted out in actual life.

When the middle zone remains fairly clear but the letters of the lower zone crowd the capitals of the next line (48) we meet the writer who seems absolutely

47 *What are you going to do at Tom Jones party*

48 *This person named Jim Smith he is fully in with Mary Jane*

normal until an emergency, a crisis or other unexpected occurrence reveals him as quite irresponsible. He is quite able to manage the daily routine, but in an emergency will undoubtedly lose his head.

SUMMARY

Average space
Able to think clearly and logically; well-balanced; an extrovert. If the spacing is uneven: chatty; gullible.

Wide space
Having an analytical mind; standing on hard facts; well-mannered; clean; considerate; reasonable; possessing the capabilities of a good executive and good organiser; having the capacity for clear presentation of complicated facts.

Too wide space
Incoherent; fearful of logical mistakes; feeble minded; having a blasé attitude.

Small spaces
Lacking reserve; spontaneous; slightly muddled in thinking; unclear about himself.

Too small spaces
Unable to see things as they really are; regressive; infantile.

Lower zone descends into next line's upper zone
Uninhibited; unable to control sexual impulses; over-occupied with instinctual life.

Upper zone reaches into preceding line's lower zone
Prone to erotic fancies, usually not acted out.

Lower zone crowds capitals of next line while middle zone remains clear
Capable of managing daily routine, but incapable of reasonable thinking and proper emotional life; apt to lose head in emergency.

Space between words

Whilst we have said that the space between lines is deliberate, we also say that the space between words is definitely non-deliberate. Even very sensitive writers have no idea whether or not they leave space between the words they write, or whether this space is large or small. Words on paper follow one after the other very much as they do in speech. A person who speaks with pauses may do so because he is accustomed to pondering and considering before he acts, or because he wants to stress each word of his calculated speech and let it sink in, or perhaps because he does not know what to say, or is overcome with emotion. He will space his words on paper **(49)**, the spacing being wide and even. On the positive side, the writer probably has an interest in literature, is fond of music and poetry. He will be an

49 *Season of mists and fruitfulness. Close bosom of the maturing sun.*

introvert with deep feeling, firmly-rooted convictions, cautious and rather critical. The negative side will be corroborated by other signs in his writing. Why is he choosing such carefully wide spaces between words? Is he, perhaps, overcome by emotion or does not know what exactly to say? The graphologist must remember that no certain trait of personality or character is shown

50 *The moving finger writes and having writ moves on. Nor all thy piety nor wit shall lure it back to cancel half a line*

51 *The writer of this script is probably conceited or is*

merely by one characteristic in the writing. There are always corroborative signs.

The spaces between words may, in some writers' hands, be found to be wide but uneven—their sizes are unequal **(50)**. Here we have the man who hesitates; who is suffering from a certain confusion; who may, indeed, be a little tricky. These, of course, are the sizeably wide spaces. In some writing the wide space appears to be grossly exaggerated **(51)**. The pauses outweigh the importance of the text, and we must conclude that the writer is conceited, affected, and probably inhibited.

Often there is little or no pause between the writer's words **(52)**. He is probably a man of action who does not make a habit of thinking twice about the same thing or pondering on it. He may even be loath to do so. He may be superficial and incapable of any deep thinking. He

2 *Here is the man of action who does not think twice about the same thing and is rather impulsive, self-confident.*

3 *Here is the man who is a little bit too gullible and has little or no musical sense.*

may also be impulsive—but he is at the same time naturally self-confident and uncritical.

Sometimes the spaces are small but uneven **(53)**, indicating a writer who is probably rather chatty and gullible. He also has little or no musical sense.

Then we have the writer who 'joins' his words—mainly with a short thread **(54)**. Though to the casual observer it may seem that the writer has been too lazy to lift the pen from the paper, this characteristic has been found quite often in the writing of executives who have that

54 *This is the executive type, the man who is a stickler for principles, probably a pedant*

persistence peculiar to their kind, of sticklers for principles and of pedants.

SUMMARY

Small even spaces
Active; reasonable; self-confident with good balance and the capacity to be a good homemaker; extroversive.

Small uneven spaces
Chatty; gullible; having little or no musical sense.

Sizeable even spaces
Interested in literature; fond of music and poetry; cautious; critical with deep feelings and firmly-rooted convictions; introversive.

Sizeable uneven spaces
Hesitant; confused; tricky.

Very wide spaces
Conceited; affected; inhibited.

Joined words
Having that persistence often found in the make-up of an executive; pedantive and a stickler for principles.

Space between letters

When we were children and we abandoned the printed letter, we were taught to connect all our letters. Some of us still do; others choose to proceed without the normal correctness, apparently feeling free to break up the single, meaningful unity of a word. This discarding of a characteristic feature of handwriting appears to signify that the writers are expressing their readiness to stand alone, to rely upon themselves. In certain occupations this trait of character is sometimes indispensable. A creative writer, an artist, an inventor must, while at work, rely upon himself.

Graphology finds that the man who relies upon himself, who can stand on his own two feet as regards creative ideas, disconnects some of his letters (55).

Independence is cherished not only by the creative person. Other people are loath to co-operate with their

55 *This man disconnects some of his letters and is rather*

56 *This man disconnects all of his letters. He is a definite individualist, maybe anti-social*

fellow men. The man who chooses to revolt against the chains which bind one member of society to the others may be a genius, an individualist, a hermit, or an anti-social neurotic. The writer revolts completely against the teachings of his childhood and writes completely unconnected letters (56).

If we want a practical and reasonable person who is a logical and systematic thinker, who is co-operative, we choose the person who connects all his letters (57), but because he has not shown any original thought of his own in letter connection, we put him down as having little initiative and a lack of intuitive thinking and acting. He is not, like the creative man, sometimes guided by

57 *This man connects all his letters. He should be logical and practical*

his emotions and, because of this, he may be a little inconsiderate.

Linked with this connection of letters, curiously enough, is the i dot. As a rule the i dot is suspended above a word, but that disturbs the fluency of the writing. A few very intelligent writers include it in the writing movement—it may connect with the letter before or after it. We find the connected i dot in the script of the integral and comprehensive thinkers, often of world stature, of great physicists, of moralists and poets.

If we look closely we see three ways of connecting the i dot with the word. The connecting link may start with the preceding letter and end with the i dot (58). It may start with the i dot and end with the following letter (59). It may connect both ways—from the preceding letter to the i dot to the following letter (60).

The first thinker approaches the problem of the i dot with an opinion intuitively conceived—he is a theorist, a philosopher, a dogmatist. The second draws his conclusions from a given case or experience (in this case the i dot) and so we say that he has the gift of integration. The third should have both an intuitive and a logical way of thinking, but as the two conflict we must think of him as having a certain inconsistency, a tendency to get stuck in an argument or problem.

It may be said here that writing where all the i dots are connected with the words is comparatively unknown —there are always some separate, as the writer connects his i dots only when and where it is reasonable.

Going back once again to when we were children, we were taught to end the last letter of a word with a flowing stroke (62). Once again some of the more intelligent among us have dispensed with this last stroke as superfluous (61). To omit such a stroke takes a special effort, for nobody can bring his pen to a dead stop without determination and self-discipline. Such a writer must have a strong will—but only in minor tasks. This, of course, amounts to obstinacy. Such a writer will have a lack of sympathy and a definite unwillingness to make concessions to sentimentality.

Occasionally one finds all the letters of a word well connected except the first (63) or the last (64). In the first case the writer pauses before he undertakes anything; he is cautious and he procrastinates. In the second case, after he has undertaken all but the last step, the writer starts pondering; he reconsiders that which has already appeared settled. When he is presented with a contract, he hesitates over signing and starts once again thinking about matters which others have thought already settled.

58–64 reading from left to right

D

Sometimes even the letters themselves are broken or seem to fall apart (65). The implication here is that a very low intelligence is at work if the clue appears in decayed or deteriorated handwriting. This phenomenon

65 *The letters are broken and*

is particularly observable in the letters **a, b, d**, and **k**. In the normal hand it is indicative of writers who are inclined to erratic, irrational acts.

SUMMARY

All letters connected
Capable of logical and systematic thinking; co-operative; reasonable; realistic; unimaginative; lacking initiative; lacking intuitive thinking and acting.

Some letters unconnected
Inventive; possessing initiative; ideas man; critical in observation and examination; individualistic; self-reliant; artistic and intuitive in thinking and acting.

Most letters unconnected
Discursive; egoistic; egocentric; moody; inconsistent; restless; selfish; shy; unsociable.

Lack of end strokes
Self-disciplined; obstinate; selfish.

First letter stands apart
Cautious; guilty of procrastination.

Last letter stands apart
Guilty of vacillating, starting to consider when every-

thing seems settled; hesitant; guilty of postponing signing of concluded contracts.

i dot connected with the first part of a word
Intuitive; capable of abstract deductive thinking; capable
of being a theoretical worker.

i dot connected with last part of a word
Having the gift of integration; capable of inductive
thinking.

i dot connected with both parts of a word
Intuitive, deductive and philosophical as well as an
integral thinker; having a tendency to intellectual
inconsistency.

Broken letters
In normal hand: having an inclination to erratic,
irrational acts. In deteriorated hand: low in intelligence,
maybe schizophrenic.

Chapter 4

Slant

THE writer's approach to other people is expressed in the slant of his handwriting, whether it is to the right, whether it is vertical or whether it is to the left—or 'backhand'. It will reveal whether he is affectionate and demonstrative, reserved and self-contained or aloof and impersonal.

People who write with a right slant (66) are the social, affectionate and demonstrative individuals who need the company of others and who choose the right kind of vocation in which they are in constant contact with their fellow men. Human relationships mean more to them than material gain. They are the extroverts and they are normally more bent upon activity than upon contemplation. Their emotions, more than their reasoning, guide them in the formation of important decisions, and they are sentimentalists.

Among their members we find the actor, the salesman, the politician, the social worker, the nurse. They are the 'joiners', and they comprise the large number who make up the social structure of society. It has also been noticed that the person in a hurry, the impatient person, and the active writer will always adopt the right slant. So will the excited and the excitable, the restless and the uninhibited. The writing of the person of conviction, aggressive but sympathetic, also slants right.

Sometimes, however, the writing leans extremely far

to the right **(67),** and here we are faced with a form of outer expression that often approaches hysteria. Such a writer cannot function adequately without other people. His writing reveals a very intense need for others, though they themselves may spurn his company. One name that stands out in this category of handwriting was Hitler.

Then there is the writer whose script leans extremely far to the left **(68).** This is beyond the normal slant of

66 *It's a long, long way*

67 *You never think I am mad to do this thing for you. The main reason*

68 *Now is the time for all good*

69 *Here is the sober man or woman who*

the reserved person. The writer is intensely emotional, but he is withdrawn, detached and undemonstrative.

Vertical writing shows us the angle of reserve. The writer is usually self-contained, calm, somewhat aloof **(69).** His emotions may be intense, but they are held in check by the mind which sits in judgement over the impulses. The majority of writers of a vertical hand have a certain charm which is the result of poise and good manners. They are often friendly in their manner but do not permit a ready intimacy on the part of others.

The vertical writer is a realist, and although sentiment may not be lacking in his nature, he often deliberately avoids showing it. He is normally selective in his choice of friends—many so-called snobs fall into this category. Depending upon the type of work he does, there may be an equal share of extroversion and introversion in a person writing a vertical hand. The actress' writing may be vertical and large, which indicates a preponderance of extroversion. The research worker's may be small, which indicates that the accent is on introversion. Very large writing in any slant indicates a good share of extroversion.

In the region of the left-slanters we find people who are repressed, aloof, inhibited and less interested in people than in things. A backhand script which is also very small reveals an interest in abstractions. Although the left-slant writer may appear friendly and communicative and may mix with other people, it is in a detached and impersonal way. Between him and the others there is always some kind of barrier. Even those close to him —his wife, his mother, his intimate friends—have difficulty in reaching him. He keeps himself barricaded, usually because of some experiences of isolation in childhood which set him apart from the others.

Women who write with a left-slant (70) frequently have a strong masculine component. They often appear elusive and something of a mystery. They may go in for adventurous episodes, and may appear cold, deliberate and impersonal. On the other hand, the left-slant male will be found to be a little feminine, fussy, a busybody eager to please and with a devotion to the ladies. He will probably be a disappointed and dissatisfied lover, though he may be slightly promiscuous. In both the male and female there is opposition to or escapism from marriage in the prevailing sense.

Some writers vary the slant even in a single line of writing. Some slant the middle zone left and the upper and lower zones upright or right (71) which indicates that the writer is intellectually and emotionally drawn

70 The female of the species is different from the male

71 How is your father there

72 My dog has got a chill, I am afraid. I am going

73 All the time I am nervous that Bill will find out

to his fellow men, but has difficulty in bringing himself to be one of them. Perhaps he has sacrificed himself for a family claim such as his mother or sister.

Then we have writing in which the lower zone is left-slanted and the upper and middle zones upright or right-slanted (72). This reveals a sexual inadequacy or resignation to an incomplete sexual life.

Sporadic left traits in upright or right-slanted writing (73) tell us that the subject possesses scepticism or distrust. The writer is a victim of inner conflicts and, if the letters are broken or split as well, he is of schizophrenic disposition.

We sometimes find left-slanted end strokes with pressure in upright or right-slanted script (74), which reveals obstinacy and stubborness. Here is the man who, whether right or wrong, takes his stand and will not be budged by either argument or threats.

There are other types of slant which reveal the degree of enthusiasm with which a writer faces his daily tasks. One may observe in some handwriting an increasing right-slant at the end of right-slanted words (75). This indicates that the subject's interest in things he undertakes grows the more he studies them. His optimism overpowers his original reserve and he is unable to hide his true intentions. He is probably hot-headed and, when excited, loses his self-control. He also probably has a quick temper.

74 *Keep on smiling, John*

75 *There's no way out for*

76 *Now is the time for you*

77 *what is the time you have*

78 *Now is the time for all*

On the other hand the right slant may grow more upright at the ends of words (76). Here the writer's pessimism overcomes his original optimism and enthusiasm. His interest in a thing lessens the more he studies it; his scepticism is stronger than his confidence. He may be an incurable pessimist.

We have already spoken of Hitler whose state of mental stability has been debated by psychiatrists and historians since before World War II. He wrote with a very exaggerated slant—more than 55 degrees—similar to that shown in (77). Beware this extreme right—

or left—slant. The writer is in all probability pathological.

There is also the handwriting which reveals a variety of slants—to the left, vertical, to the right (78). One can accurately conclude that the writer is yanked in many directions—just like his script. Sometimes he is sociable and spontaneous; at other times withdrawn, self-contained. Occasionally he may go into his shell completely. He is mercurial, unstable, unpredictable, difficult to pin down. He may be depressed or anxious.

SUMMARY

Right slant
Female: Agreeable; sympathetic; affectionate; hearty; optimistic; possessing strong sympathies and antipathies.

Male: Optimistic; spontaneous; having initiative and strong sympathies and antipathies together with a drive for independence; ambitious; agressive; courageous; idealistic; having a pioneering spirit; impetuous; affectionate; being a humanitarian and an advocate of marriage in the prevailing sense.

Increasing right slant at end of words
Having an interest in a thing which grows the more he studies it; being unable to hide his true intentions; having optimism which overpowers his original reserve; hotheaded; when excited losing self-control; quicktempered.

Diminishing right slant at end of words
Having an interest in a thing which lessens the more he studies it; having pessimism which overcomes his original enthusiasm, and scepticism stronger than confidence; incurably pessimistic.

Sporadic left traits in upright or right-slanted writing

Sceptical; distrustful; being a victim of inner conflicts (with split letters—being of schizophrenic disposition).

Very right slant, more than 55 degrees

Mixed up mentally and emotionally; could be pathological.

Upright

Reasonable; lacking sentimentality; sober; reserved; aloof; mature; critical; having good concentration; impartial; temperate; reliable; cool-headed; introspective; self-centred; frugal.

Left slant

Female: Independent; bold; cold-blooded; clever; ambitious; egoistic; selfish; man-hating; promiscuous; cynical; having opposition to marriage in the prevailing sense.

Male: Feminine; sentimental; tender; domestic; busybody-minded; diligent; petty; fussy; being a homebody; eager to please; devoted to the ladies; being always a disappointed and dissatisfied lover; promiscuous; sexually inverted; averse to marriage in the prevailing sense; sarcastic; supercilious.

Middle zone left-slanted, upper zone and lower zone upright or right-slanted

Intellectually and emotionally drawn to fellow men but having difficulty in bringing himself to be one of them. May be sacrificing himself for family claim, such as mother or sister.

Lower zone left-slanted, upper and middle zones upright or right-slanted

Sexually inadequate or resigned to an incomplete sexual life.

Left-slanted heavy end strokes in upright or right-slanted writing
Obstinate; sticking to his own opinions whether right or wrong.

Size

We say that the size of a script is indicative of how the writer sees the world. If the script is large, then he gets the full, broad picture; if it is small, then it seems as if he is looking at things as through a microscope—he sees the detail. But this is only a generality.

Like any other design on paper, a letter may extend in four directions: up, down, to the right and to the left. A 'tall' letter has a mainly up-down direction, a 'wide' letter a left-right direction. But a letter may be both tall and wide, or too tall in comparison to its width, too wide in comparison to its height.

79 *Intelligence and Pride here ½ may a Dreamer and rather Religious*

80 *What are you going to do*

81 *Here the Capitals reach into the lower zone. Is he a*

Tall capitals which extend themselves beyond the proportionately established height of the upper zone (79) are typical of the person who is superior to the rest of his fellow men, of the one who would like to be superior, and of the one who has his head in the clouds. The proud and the religious, the farsighted and the visionary, the magnanimous and the pretenders, the independent and the haughty all use tall capitals.

If the letters which occupy the middle zone—a, c, e, etc —are disproportionately tall (80), they demonstrate a desire for greatness. They also imply a certain over-emphasis and overrating of the practical and senti-mental aspects of life. They are one of the features in handwriting which betoken the feminine angle, and they crop up in the script of people who think they and their daily work ought to receive more recogni-tion. These tall minimum letters are also found in the script of writers who like a well-kept, cosy home, good food, the assurance of plenty. They are found in the handwriting of people with social standing. Curiously enough, a state of depression causes these letters to be depressed; good news makes them grow.

Capitals may also extend themselves into the lower zone (81). In such cases the writer's intention is to take hold of, to understand the instinctual or the unconscious. These capitals have been observed in the handwriting of poets, painters, musicians, authors whose themes are man's soul, his dreams, his musical sense or his sub-merged traditions, including the mystic and the mysterious. People who employ psychology in their daily occupation—physicians, social workers, psycholo-gists—are also often seen to employ this type of capital.

Letters which naturally occupy both the middle and the lower zone, such as the p, q, g, may reach down into the upper zone of the next line (82). If they are without pressure they are indicative of a certain anti-intellectual

82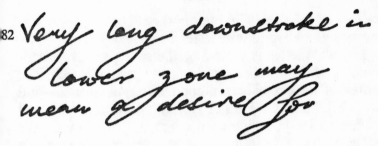
Very long downstroke in lower zone may mean a desire for

83 *This writer is dull and modest. He writes small Capitals.*

84 *What is the new date for the meeting?*

and unintellectual outlook cultivated by crass realists, by materialists, by 100 per cent businessmen. But if they have pressure we can assume that the writer is after a more tangible sense of gratification. Athletes and dancers are among those who show an extreme extension of the lower zone with pressure.

At the other end of the scale, we come across the small capitals (83) which are typical of the modest person, the person who concentrates on facts, not on ideas. He is what we call a good, reliable worker, a realist who prefers to collect facts rather than to invent.

Small minimum letters show us the worker who has the power of concentration, who is frugal—and masculine (84). First-rate research workers, thinkers, teachers, scientists have been seen to write these small minimum letters. They are keeping themselves under the strictest self-control in order to be able to accomplish what they undertake. But it should also be noted that feelings of inferiority and temporary depression are also shown by small minimum letters.

The wide letter is typical of the spontaneous, broad-minded writer who is sociable and sympathetic **(85)**. The writer is an extrovert, a good teller of stories—and probably boastful. He is eager to share with you and willing to let you share with him. Often, though, the letter is too wide **(86)** and when we see this sign, we suspect that the writer is obtrusive, impudent, perhaps just plain nosey.

Lean handwriting, on the other hand, marks the reasonable, critical, sober and also unimaginative **(87)** and because the writer is unimaginative, he is probably also inartistic. He is an introvert, economical, perhaps inhibited and narrow-minded. Often he is plain unsociable. If the letter is too narrow **(88)**, the subject is

85 *is imagination*
artistic talent

86 *I am just*

87 *This writer is reasonable and*
He may be rather cool and ???

88 *This writing is far too narrow. The writer is probably timid ot*

probably timid, seclusive, suspicious and, in many cases, avaricious.

We often see narrow letters widely spaced, or wide letters which follow closely upon one another. Obviously there is a contradiction here. Narrow letters widely spaced reveal one whose sympathy and generosity are either pretence or forced upon him by circumstance.

89 *These loops widen backward.*
I have a mother fixation

90 *These loops widen foward*
I have a father fixation

Wide letters narrowly spaced are characteristic of the liberal and sympathetic person whom circumstances force to be economical and concentrated.

There may be a widening tendency to the left **(89)**, which indicates the writer's desire to include the past and the mother in his daily routine. He is guilty of regression, not progression. If, on the other hand, the widening tendency is to the right **(90)**, there is a father fixation here—the writer is looking outward and forward.

There is a great significance in the first and the last letter of a word. The first letter shows us the writer's front, the way he looks at us and wants to be looked at, his intentions and also his pretensions. The last letter betrays the decision the writer has arrived at, his final standpoint. If we wish to determine the writer's bearing, his initiative, his intelligence, we must examine his initials. Whether or not and how he carries out his intentions, whether he is reliable and co-operative or just arrogant is expressed in the size, legibility and form of the last letter.

A clear, well-proportioned last letter (91) indicates a clear and trustworthy decision. An illegible, neglected or omitted last letter (92) can be taken to be just the opposite—and is a warning. A very tall last letter (93) tells us that the writer not only has an opinion but insists upon it, because he has either character, or is opinionated and arrogant. If the last letter is smaller than the rest, we see a tendency to yield; what may seem to a stranger to

91 *what are we to do for now that Jack has*

92 *When are we to manan ann*

93 *This is my opinion*

94 *and so to bed*

95 *and so to bed*

be lack of backbone is really due to human understanding.

There are a few inconsistent qualities which occur in some scripts. One of them is the sort of tall, wide letters, right-slanted, without pressure, (94). Here we have a lack of concentration, a lack of reserve. There may be impatience and lack of thoroughness as with the

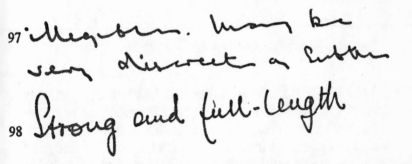

96 *These letters are small and written with pressure. They*

dreamer, the schemer, the undisciplined and reckless person.

Tall, wide and left-slanted without pressure (95), and we have the person who simulates generosity, sympathy and sociability, and who might be called by his friends slightly two-faced.

Small letters with heavy pressure (96) show slowness,

97 *illegible... may be very discreet a hidden*

98 *Strong and full-length*

heaviness, at times excitability and explosiveness—together with inhibition.

When there is a lack of uniformity in letters, some large, some small, we must conclude that the writer views life with some inconsistency. He is changeable and may even be a little shifty.

Sometimes we find the script almost illegible, using threads instead of letters **(97)**. Here we have the shrewd man, discreet and diplomatic and not always sincere. This type of man will adapt himself to almost any situation where he can gain. An opportunist—but not necessarily a dishonest one.

The strong and full-length downstroke **(98)** is found in the writing of a man who is a leader. He has the ability to conceive ideas or at least take the initiative, and the will and capacity to carry out what is under-

99 *Give the dog a big bone*
Mary has dug a very

100 *This long downstroke is left-*
slanted in a right-slanted

101 *Very weak downstroke*
with heavy left-right

taken. He is upright, reliable but headstrong and may frequently be difficult to deal with because he is somewhat stiff and inflexible. He is a thorough worker provided his personal interests go with the job in hand, and he is willing to fight for his beliefs. His most unshakable belief is in himself.

If the downstroke is disproportionately long in the lower zone **(99)** we find a desire for sexual satisfaction—and an inversely proportionate capacity for finding it. A long downstroke, left-slanted in right-slanted script **(100)**, is often found in the writing of people who have an opposition to or frustration with regard to sexual intercourse. Then there is the very weak downstroke which is combined with heavy left-right strokes **(101)**. We have here heavy lapses of potency, perhaps with a psychological cause. And because the sexual inadequacy is bound to have its effect upon the psychology of the individual, we may have a vicious circle.

SUMMARY

Wide script
Imaginative; warm; with artistic talent; spontaneous; courageous; having initiative and being a good teller of stories and good mixer; boastful; given to fantasy; perhaps insincere.

Lean script
Reasonable; critical; objective; cool; perhaps stern or harsh.

Tall capitals
Intelligent; ambitious; having the spirit of enterprise; far sighted; independent; religious; proud; idealistic; having the will to dominate though perhaps a dreamer.

Small capitals
Dull; stern; docile; thorough; realistic; modest.

Tall and lean capitals and initials
Socially timid; professionally jealous; having ambition without adequate imagination; sober; cool.

Tall and wide capitals and initials
Imaginative; broadminded; artistically talented; perhaps a little muddle-headed and boastful.

Last letter taller
Ready to defend own convictions; arrogant; lacking
sensitivity to others.

Last letter smaller
Having a tendency to yield; human understanding often
mistaken for lack of backbone.

Last letter illegible, carelessly written or omitted
Not always willing or able to finish task undertaken;
having mental reservations; indecisive; cannot be relied
upon to keep his word.

Capitals reach into lower zone
Intellectually interested in the unconscious, as with
poets, musicians, authors, artists, psychologists.

Lower zone long-looped letters with pressure
Sensual; athletic; fond of dancing, swimming, walking;
having an interest in nature.

Lower zone long-looped letters without pressure
Realistic; possessing business acumen and a money
complex.

Lower zone long and wide loops
Backward widening: Mother fixation.
Forward widening: Father fixation.

Strong and full-length downstroke
Able to conceive ideas or at least take the initiative, and
having the will and capacity to carry out what is undertaken; headstrong; frequently difficult to deal with;
upright, though perhaps stiff and inflexible; reliable and
thorough in working so long as personal interests go
with job on hand; willing to fight for beliefs.

Disproportionately long downstroke in lower zone
Desiring sexual satisfaction but having an inversely proportionate capacity for finding it.

Long downstroke left-slanted in right-slanted script
Experiencing opposition to or frustration with regard to sexual intercourse.

Very weak downstroke where there are heavy left-right strokes
Lapsing into impotency very often.

Writing which is almost illegible and uses threads instead of letters
Shrewd; discreet; diplomatic; subtle; not always sincere; able to adapt himself to almost any situation where he can gain, although not necessarily dishonest; being an opportunist.

Tall and wide letters without pressure, right-slanted
Lacking concentration; lacking reserve; lacking thoroughness; impatient; scheming; dreaming; undisciplined; reckless.

Tall and wide letters without pressure, left-slanted
Simulating generosity and sociability.

Small letters with pressure
Slow; excitable; explosive; inhibited.

Chapter 5

Connecting strokes

THE connection of letters facilitates the process of writing. To write fluently and spontaneously we must join the letters. Thinking also involves connecting. To think and act logically we must connect our thoughts with one another. As soon as we know how a person connects his thoughts we have a notion of his way of thinking and we know him pretty well. With a good deal of accuracy we can predict his attitude and often his actions.

Graphology undertakes to interpret the writer's idea of co-operation on the basis of his letter connection. There are three widely used links—the garland, the arcade and the angle. In addition there are three less widely used links—the thread, the S-link and the shark's tooth.

THE GARLAND takes the form of a platter, a cup or a calix. It is the most practical, quick, easy method of connecting two letters. The shallower the garland, the quicker and easier the writing (102). We are likely to see the garland in the writing of the enthusiastic dancer and traveller, the mobile and the elusive, the peaceable and the easy going.

There are writers who pen their garlands like a platter (103). They are understood to be receptive to anything new; they are 'open for suggestions'. They do not shut themselves away from the world. They are not plotters, not hermits, but neither are they abstract thinkers. They are rather the progressive and outdoor types who hate being fenced in. But both the open-mindedness and the hospitality have something of the exhibitionist in them. They are demonstrative, even shallow and indiscriminate at times.

The garlands may be deeper and more cuplike (104), which indicate the kind-hearted and the sympathetic, also the collector of rarities or common stamps, of valuables or trifles. Because of these qualities the garland is thought to be the preferred letter connection

102 *~~~~~~*

103 *Flat garlands may*

104 *These garlands*

105 *Depression overcomes me*

of female or feminine writers. The writer of cuplike garlands may be basically conservative—even narrow minded—sedate, quiet, contemplative, and perhaps complacent.

Really deep calix-like garlands (105) are to be found in the writing of the depressively minded who have a tendency to take everything tragically. These people, too, are contemplative and sedate and they have a deep and feminine sympathy for the needy and the helpless.

Superfluous garlands, such as flourishes (106), indicate that the writer possesses calculated amiability in order to ingratiate himself with people. There are also what is known as the enclosing garlands where there are an unnecessary number of loops or whorls (107). They

106 *Superfluous*

107 *Yours sincerely*

108 *Square garlands are*

109 *This man may be a hypocrite or he may*

indicate mental reservations, unspontaneous and narrow mindedness. Square garlands (108) indicate strict conventionality, narrow mindedness, rejection of instinctual drives. The writer could well be described as a 'stuffed shirt'.

Certain letters such as the **a**, **o**, **u**, **d**, and **b** have a garland-like base. If this base has an unexpected and irregular opening (109), we should be on our guard against criminal tendencies in the writer. Such writing has been seen in the hands of murderers and swindlers —but take heed. Graphological ethics do not permit one to mention criminal tendencies unless there are in the script some other indications of similar import.

THE ARCADE is the garland turned upside down. As a form of movement it is slower than the garland, and it presupposes a writer who keeps his eyes open, who has a good sense of proportion, who knows instinctively what to aim at and where to land. The arcade writer relies upon his instinct and intuition rather than reason.

He is always trying to hide something, but that in itself does not mean anything. He may be a sinister plotter, an artist who goes his own way, or a conscientious official hiding important documents entrusted to his care.

The more arched the arcade **(110)** the more prominent become its artistic qualities. Flat arcades **(111)** have been

110 *High arcades may mean poise and pride and*

111 *Flat arcades may mean this man is a schemer*

found in the writing of hypocrites and intriguers. But make sure you avoid serious error—they are easily overlooked or mistaken for garlands.

THE ANGLE is made with not one but two movements, and the abrupt gestures which produce the angle are without grace, flexibility or the spirit of reconciliation **(112)**. We think of angle writers as people who are willing to submit themselves to a rigid discipline and who are prepared to impose such a discipline on their environment. They are reliable, firm, steadfast and imperturbable—but they are also in some cases dull, heavy, brutal, not to be stopped. The angle writer will also be rather unyielding, intolerant, cold, pitilessly logical. Principles are more to him that individual considerations; the method often more important than the result. His aim is reason, not humaneness. We conceive him capable of abstract thinking, of technological discoveries—but also of cunning.

112　*John Smith is an angle*

113　*small, quick and firm*

114　*small and change*

115　*angles with heavy*

Small, quick but firm angles **(113)**, indicate the reliable and imperturbable worker. Angles with a frequently changing slant **(114)**, tell us of irritability and excitability, of suspicion and inner conflicts. The writer who pens his angles with a heavy pressure **(115)**, has fighting spirit, is vehement and domineering. When he is in the wrong job—a square peg in a round hole—he is querulous and restless.

Few individuals can maintain one type of link throughout their writing. Many writers mix angles and garlands and, more rarely, arcades **(116)**. This complicates the task of interpretation, but it also makes it more fruitful, for such writers are the people of whom every

116　*and now that you have come*

117　*you have to go now if you*

118　*This shows avarice or greed*

acquaintance gives a different description. If the various links are not firmly and clearly executed **(117)**, we have writers who cannot make up their minds. Firm execution is indicative of the writer's willingness to stand up for his social convictions. Narrow, small angles **(118)**, show strong emotional inhibition. There will probably, too, be a touch of avarice, both in the financial sense and as regards possessions.

THREADS stand alone in their execution, for no link is so easily, quickly and carelessly made as a thread. Sober realists and pedants would not feel at ease with such a connection **(119)**. It lacks form and character and backbone, and it seems to belong to one who received his impressions and counsel from everywhere, whose hysterical ambiguity and many-sidedness escape definition. Quick threads without pressure have been found in the script of confidence men and people who, if need be, can sympathise with anybody—in other words, opportunists. They are also found in the hands of people who do not stand up for their convictions, who know how to turn almost everything to account, and who cannot be pinned down. There are threads which show pressure. Such writers refuse to be chained to definite and traditional rules because they want to be free to follow their talents, their instincts, and what they believe to be their destiny. When the thread points to the lower zone it indicates an instinctual lawlessness. When it points to the upper zone, it shows a high intelligence with an excellent gift of integration.

THE S-LINK is a variation of the thread **(120)**. It is interpreted as the occasional tool of those who rely on their instinct and intuition to guide them. They have ambitious aims which they pursue instinctively and, so to speak, blindly without much regard for bourgeois considerations. They are excellent negotiators, adaptable

119 *thand*

120 *Here One Goes To*

121 **Here are shark's teeth**

to any circumstance. S-links occur in all three zones and both at the beginning and end of a word, so the interpretation must, of course, consider zone and location.

THE SHARK'S TOOTH looks like an angle, but it is not an angle. It is easily overlooked in handwriting, but it appears exactly as the name conveys (121). It is characteristic of people whose business it is to profit, broadly speaking, from other people's credulity. The business may not be illegal—shark's teeth are often found in the writing of women who are able to outsmart everyone, particularly their friends and husbands. Whenever a naïve person and a shark's tooth writer meet, the former is in for a cutting and cut-up experience.

SUMMARY

Deep garlands
Depressive; tending to take everything tragically; possessing a deep feminine sympathy for the needy and helpless; contemplative; sedate.

Flat garlands
Similar to the practiced businessman who wants to proceed without friction; conventionally amiable; having

obliging manners; mobile; boastful; reckless; unconcerned; inconsiderate.

Square garlands
Strictly conventional; rejecting instinctual drives; narrow minded.

Enclosing garlands
Mentally reserved; practiced in unspontaneous and calculated 'kindnesses'; scheming; narrow minded.

Superfluous garlands such as flourishes
Practising calculated amiability in order to ingratiate himself with people.

Garlandlike lower part of letters open at the base
Criminal tendencies. Watch also for other indications such as ambiguous letters, arcades, irregular over-elaborate flourishes, irregular spotty blotches.

High arcades
Inward; self-sufficient; poised; proud; reserved; profound; artistically gifted.

Flat arcades
Hypocritical; guilty of skilful and unobtrusive scheming.

Small, quick but firm angles
Reliable; imperturbable in working habits.

Angles with frequently changing slant
Irritable; excitable; prone to inner conflicts.

Angles with heavy pressure
Possessing a fighting spirit; vehement; guilty of brutal opposition; domineering. (When vocationally misplaced, querulous, restless.)

Narrow, small angles
Emotionally inhibited; avaricious.

Threads without pressure
Hasty or muddle-headed; guilty of being a confidence man or a person who can, if need be, understand and sympathise with everyone; opportunistic; can't be pinned down; guilty of never standing up for his own convictions; knowing how to turn almost everything to account.

Threads with pressure
Refusing to be chained to definite and traditional rules because of a wish to be free to follow own talents and instincts; creative; able instinctively to do the right thing—for himself; refusing to acknowledge fetters.

S-links
Capable of relying on instinct and intuition for guidance; having ambitious aims which are pursued instinctively and blindly without much regard for bourgeois considerations; excellent in negotiation; adaptable to any circumstance. (Interpretation must consider zone and locality.)

Shark's tooth
Very smart; possessing the capacity for profiting from other people's credulity.

Concealing, diagonal and counter strokes

We now go on to another important point in handwriting which gives a valuable clue to the graphologist—the concealing stroke. It is not seen at first glance and the unsuspecting reader will very likely overlook it, yet it has its own peculiar value. If we make a pen stroke and then another which conceals it, the reader will appreciate just how difficult is detection.

In graphology the concealing stroke is the well-known sign of inhibition. It is coupled very often with insincerity, and it is difficult to see where one leaves off and the other begins. There is probably no insincerity which is not caused by some inhibition, and no inhibition without some insincerity to help the writer rationalise and justify it. The socially timid, too, feel the need to bolster their bearing with a concealing stroke, probably in the first letter of a word, particularly in the signature. Other varieties of concealing stroke may be interpreted by observing the zone in which they appear, or they may be found in the garland, the arcade or the angle.

122 *bully for you*

123 *and now I have to go*

124 *what folly you have*

125 *and I am socially*

126 *Patrick Taylor*

Because the concealing stroke can and does hide something bad and weak, we cannot interpret it without considering the general appearance of the script. The concealing stroke in the upper zone (122), implies secrecy about the writer's plans and ideas. In the middle zone generally (123), we get the impression of emotional delusions, exaggerated or compulsive taciturnity at times.

The lower zone takes in the unconscious or the instinctual and when we see a concealing stroke there (124), we know that the writer clamps down on or is secretive about facts in his instinctual life. The socially timid usually make use of a concealing stroke in the middle zone of the first letter of a word (125). It seems as though, initially, they are afraid to join and mix and only their own willpower helps them eventually to join the throng despite their fear of social contact. The socially timid is almost always introversive, perhaps through some psychological trauma in early life. If the concealing stroke appears in the capitals (126), we see

127 *lessons*

128 *fig leaf*

129 *I'll meet*

130 *Thread*

a certain amount of frustrated ambition from either psychological or physical causes.

The habitual liar and the crafty embezzler both employ concealing strokes with their arcades **(127)**, and the shrewd and sly use it with their angles **(128)**.

Then there is the concealing stroke in garlands **(129)**, which indicates constraint, shyness, emotional inhibitions. In threads **(130)**, it indicates a refusal to take a stand or be pinned down, a certain amount of deception.

THE DIAGONAL STROKE may be an upstroke or a downstroke, and though the two appear on the surface to be

131 *And now, what*

132 *peaceful und*

133 *And now what*

the same, there is a subtle difference. The upstroke is going from a lower zone to a higher one, the downstroke from a higher to a lower. The diagonal stroke in **(131)**, an upstroke, has been found in the script of argumentative writers. Since it comes from the emotional realm and heads into the conscious, it must be assumed that the writer wishes to air a problem of emotional origin. We tend to be stubborn, excited, unwilling to listen when our emotions are deeply involved, so this stroke is nearly always indicative of a rather irrational argumentativeness. On the other hand, a similar stroke executed as a downstroke **(132)**, traverses its path from the conscious (middle zone) to the unconscious (lower zone) and, according to most leading graphologists, does not imply

F

argumentativeness because the path it takes is the path from articulation to muteness.

The diagonal stroke may, of course, start in the middle zone and continue to the upper zone **(133)**. We can say that its purpose is not an irrational argument for emotional reasons but the assertion of intentions, not contentions. It is the businessman's upstroke—the man who wants to further matters, not complicate them.

THE COUNTERSTROKE is not primarily a stroke—the accent is on the 'counter' quality, the contrariness. It may sometimes be an opening where a continuous line is expected, or an arcade where a garland ought to be. It may be a left tending stroke instead of a right tending stroke, or a downstroke where you can expect an up-stroke.

The counterstroke is the sign of the person who is stamped with amorality, the writer who shows active resistance to the normal, the legal and the accepted. It has been seen not only in the hands of bluffers and boastful people, but in the hands of thieves, forgers and embezzlers. Here it must be said that a great deal of harm can be done by a false accusation, and it is most advisable not to base that accusation on any one sign of moral corruption.

SUMMARY

Concealing strokes

In the first letter of a word. Middle zone: Socially timid; Capitals: Frustrated in his ambition.

In upper zone generally: Secretive about plans and ideas.

In middle zone generally: Suffering from emotional

delusions; prone to exaggerated or compulsive taciturnity.

In lower zone generally: Secretive about instinctual life.

In garlands: Constrained; shy; prone to emotional inhibitions.

In arcades: Capable of shrewd restraint or sly lying and hypocrisy.

In angles: Shrewd; capable of being a confidence man.

In threads: Deceptive; refusing to take a stand or be pinned down.

Typical counterstrokes

Arcade where there should be a garland (134). Downstroke which should be upstroke (135). Left tending which should be right tending (136). Opening at the base of letters (137). Garlands instead of arcades (138).

134 *with*

135 *β*

136 *I leads*

137 *hour by hour*

138 *mannerism*

Diagonal strokes

Starting from lower zone: Argumentative (perhaps irrationally so).

Starting from upper zone as a downstroke: Preferring not to argue but to stay silent in a discussion which involves emotional feelings.

Starting from middle zone and proceeding to upper: Peculiar to the businessman, the man who makes an assertion of intentions not contentions, whose intention is to further matters not to complicate them.

Chapter 6

Capitals

CAPITAL letters often form the 'face' which we show to society. The way we write them gives important clues towards our tastes, pride and feeling towards authority. They also tell whether we are vain, conceited, egoistic, modest, self-effacing, humble, old fashioned, artistic or just plain vulgar. The larger the capital, the greater the pride. Small capitals indicate modesty, self-effacement, often humility.

The way a writer pens the capital **I** tells something specific about his opinion of himself as well as what he wants others to think of him. It reveals the kind of intellect he has, gives a clue to his talents and, together with his signature, discloses whether he has an inferiority complex of one kind or another and has found compensation for it.

The capital **A** with the initial stroke tells us that the person uses this stroke almost as a prop to give him pause in a situation before expressing himself—he is cautious. The second **A**, which is open at the top, shows generosity. The third **A**, neat and orderly, is written by a neat, orderly, methodical, reliable person **(139)**.

On occasions one meets the person with a carefree attitude towards life. He may be level-headed in serious matters, but is apt to overlook important details. His **A** has an unnecessary extension to the horizontal bar **(140)**.

Looped horizontal strokes in the **A (141)**, show musical awareness. The writer is a colourful personality.

There are four types of **B** in **(142)**. The extra inflated stroke on the left of No 1 shows some inflation of the ego, as does any exaggeration in the capital letters. **B** No 2 is open at the base, telling us that the writer is generous. **B** No 3 is closed at the base, indicating caution. **B** No 4 has no horizontal stroke, and reveals a neat,

139–144 reading from left to right

orderly mind, but the writer feels slightly inferior and is apt to lack the courage of his own convictions. He finds himself unable to make a snap decision in a crisis.

Then we sometimes meet the one-track mind, the person with great powers of concentration, the determined one with willpower and the ability to see a problem through from start to finish. The horizontal strokes in his **B** are almost as long behind as the curved ones in front **(143)**.

There are three **C**s in **(144)**. The initial stroke on No 1 means the same as any initial stroke on a capital letter

—a prop for the writer. The rounded **C** shows idealism and grace. The angular **C** indicates that the writer is somewhat rigid. This should be corroborated by other angular strokes in the handwriting. Four types of **D** are shown in **(145)**. No 1, which is open at the top, shows

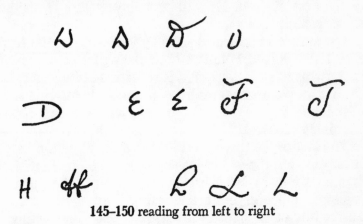

145–150 reading from left to right

frankness—and the writer of it may find it hard to keep confidences. Like its open mouth, it is a sign of talkativeness. Conversely, the closed capital **D** indicates reserve and the ability to keep a secret. The writer also keeps his own counsel and does not always reveal what he is thinking. He dislikes probing on the part of others. Sometimes we see a capital **D** with a flying loop at the top, as in No 3. This reveals a certain capriciousness. In women it may amount to coquettishness; in men flirtatiousness. There is frivolity somewhere in the nature. The fourth **D** tells us that the writer is somewhat lazy, and because it is open at the top we get the idea that he talks without thought of the consequences.

The **D** with the long horizontal strokes behind **(146)** means the same as the **B** with the long strokes to the left—a one-track mind, determined, with good powers of concentration.

Two types of **E (147)**—the rounded one for a gentle nature; the angular for a rigid nature.

The type of **F** which is the conventional form we were taught to make at school is rather ornate, and tells us that the writer likes fancy things which are not always in the best of taste. He will probably make a **T** in the same fashion **(148)**.

The simple **H** indicates simplicity of tastes and a firm ego. The involved **H** tells us that the writer gets himself into involved situations, and is something of a strategist so that he eventually gets himself out of them. This **H** is also found in the script of people who are somewhat conniving **(149)**.

The first of the three **Ls (150)** has an inflated top loop. It tells us that the writer is generous. When it is inflated at the base as in No 2 it expresses vanity. The third **L** is simple, graceful and artistic. It will usually be corroborated by other signs of artistic trends in the writing.

The letter **M** seems to be the most widely varied in the capital alphabet. There are three shown in **(151)**. The incurve of No 1 tells us that the writer has family pride and is sensitive. The graceful first stroke of No 2 indi-

151

152

153

154

cates good nature, a desire to be friendly. No 3 reveals an aesthetic sense, a liking for simple more than ornate things.

Coarse and ungraceful, the first M here **(152)**, tells us that the writer is also coarse and vulgar. In No 2 the first stroke is higher than the other two. This reveals independence and self-respect. When the first stroke is very much higher as in No 3 it tells us that the writer is opinionated and arrogant. The fourth M has the second stroke higher than the other two. This reveals a lack of tact. The fifth M, with the last stroke higher than the other two, tells us that the writer has the need to be in a position of authority in order to feel adequate. There is a slight feeling of inferiority and a drive for independence.

Simple capitals such as these **(153)** betoken a neat and orderly mind. The very extended M **(154 No 1)**, reveals diplomacy and finesse. It also reveals a tendency to waste. The second M indicates kindness, friendliness. The third and fourth are written by the creative, artistic, original and cultured writer.

Here are two Os **(155)**. The simple, closed circle shows clear, balanced thinking. The one open at the top shows frankness as in the open D, and like the open D it indicates an inability to keep a secret.

Inflation of ego is shown in the capital P as in the B already illustrated. The simple Q, like the simple O, indicates balanced and clear thinking **(156)**.

Many writers use the printed S which is the indication of constructive thinking. The second S reveals the simplicity of a person who is mentally lazy **(157)**.

Three Is are illlustrated **(158)**. All three are used by people of highly-developed intellect. The capital I made like a Roman numeral tells us that the writer is constructive and capable of clear thinking. There is some severity in his thinking—and perhaps in his taste. The

155–159 reading from left to right

second capital **I** is just a downstroke with a little cap on it. The writer thinks concisely while keeping a lid on his thoughts, not saying all of what he thinks. The single stroke of the third **I** tells us that the writer's mind can be clear and concise. The ego is strong and firm and the thought process is somewhat masculine in that it does not concern itself with detail but comes down to essentials.

Beware the Is shown in **(159)**. They start from left to right instead of from right to left. They are counterstrokes and belong to the rebel who starts out resenting parental authority and who may often later come to grips with the law. He may be a genius—but only if his writing shows capacity for self-discipline and a certain balance.

Loops

Now let us take the formation of loops. The upper loops —those which form part of the **b**, the **h**, and the **l**—give us a clue to the person's ideals and his world of fantasy. A wide upper loop is penned by a person who expresses himself through his emotions in one way or another. Musicians and singers make wide upper loops; so do people who rely more on their emotions than on their intellect. That does not mean, of course, that all intensely emotional people make this type of upper loop. Much will depend upon corroborating signs. Emotional people are very sensitive and in their handwriting you will probably see loops in the small letter **d** and often in the stem of the **t**.

When the heart is physically affected, as in a coronary or in a defective heartbeat, the upper loops often show a ragged stroke at the top. Sometimes there is a break at the top of the loop. Many people do not know, without a thorough medical check-up, that heart trouble may exist. This sign, repeated consistently, gives the graphologist a chance to sound a note of warning.

The upper loop may be compressed, not open. This indicates repression, often tenseness. The writer is also secretive about his own plans and ideas. Then there is the loop that is no loop at all—the single stroke. In the same handwriting you will probably discover other simplified letters. The writer has learned to eliminate unnecessary detail and can come down to essentials— he has a developed intellect. If in the script there are one or two such strokes present as well as other loops, one can assume that the writer is in the process of developing mentally, and may in time eliminate all other loops. Sometimes one comes across a loop that is squared at the top. This angular formation points to a measure of rigidity amounting to obstinacy. The loop that looks as if its back is broken is a sign of emotional sickness. Handwriting is an unconscious gesture which represents the strivings of the individual. Upward-reaching loops symbolise a dream world so that the very high loop tells us, particularly if it is wide and quite exaggerated, that the writer is visionary and lives a great deal in a world of fantasy.

One also comes across the low upper loop, not much higher than the small letters. The writer who pens this is close to earth, lacks imagination, is practical and rather humble. The lower loops express the instinctual, materialistic demands made upon an individual by his own nature. Long, wide, heavy lower loops indicate that the writer's physical urges are strong. This includes the sexual drive.

Then there is the lower loop which, like its counterpart in the upper zone, is not a loop at all but a single downstroke in the lower zone. The **y** looks like a 7 and the **g** looks like a 9. They are often written by people who enjoy dealing with figures. These people have practical, good judgment. Obstinacy is found in the writer of the lower zone loop which is squared, though he may also have some mechanical ability.

Let us take the variations in the loops individually.

160   Normally high **(160)**: idealistic.

161   Very high **(161)**: prone to creating fantasies; dreamer.

162   Very round **(162)**: sensitive, emotional, perhaps musical.

163   Compressed **(163)**: repressed, cautious, secretive.

164   *l*   Broken back **(164)**: emotionally sick (but watch for corroborative signs).

165   *l*   Ragged at top or even broken **(165)**: suffering from heart trouble.

166   *h*   Low loop **(166)**: unimaginative, humble.

167 *b. h. L.*   No loop **(167)**: uncluttered thinking.

168 *l h*   Squared loop **(168)**: rigid, obstinate, aggressive.

169   *y*   Long loop with pressure **(169)**: possessing a sense of the dramatic, and healthy physical appetites including sexual impulses; athletic; fond of dancing, swimming, walking. Long loop without pressure: searching for security; having a money complex.

170 *y g*   Angular **(170)**: obstinate, aggressive.

171   Like figures (171): possessing good judgement and mathematical ability.

172   Tied in knots (172): persistent, almost compulsively so.

173   Short loops (173): physical weakness.

174   Upstrokes to right instead of left (174): having the need to contribute something; having sympathy with the needy.

175   Broken lower loop (175): perhaps impaired as regards legs or feet.

176   Exaggerated wide loops (176): egoistic.

177   Return stroke to left (177): clannish.

178   Upstrokes to right rising well up (178): sarcastic.

Tied in knot **(179)**: secretive.

g like figure 8 **(180)**: capable of being a good talker, adaptable, with literary tastes.

Loop that is not really looped **(181)**: austere.

Return stroke to left **(182)**: quick in mind with fluent thought.

Stem of **d** and **t** looped **(183)**: sensitive, susceptible to flattery.

e Finals and other small letters

Watch how a person forms his small letters. They show whether he has developed habits of obedience to ordered routine, how closely he has continued to follow the lessons he first learned. Quite a number of writers stick closely to the methods taught at school, for they seem to feel safe when operating within a framework of obedience. Then they do not have to make important decisions nor accept adult responsibility.

There are others who express their individuality and

their quest for freedom by breaking away from the letter forms they were taught and developing a style of their own. Formations that were not taught in the classroom indicate a certain talent. The small letters tell us whether the writer is generous, cautious, gullible, reticent or talkative. Tightly closed, the letters spell out caution; if there is an openness at the top they tell of generosity. Sometimes, in the case of the **a** and **o** open at the top, they reveal talkativeness. Some people never simplify the strokes they were taught to make. They stick to the rules. Others, more mentally progressive, leave out unnecessary strokes and come down to essentials. Here is a variety of small letters and their meanings.

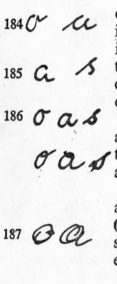

184

185

186

187

188

The **o**s and **a**s open at the top and the **s** open at the base **(184)** indicate generosity in the writer when his emotions become involved. They tell us that he shows a tendency to be talkative. The same letters closed tightly **(185)**, indicate tact and diplomacy.

If they are not only closed tightly but are knotted to make doubly sure **(186)**, the writer is usually extremely reserved and he is always secretive.

Should the **a**s and **o**s be fortified with a double wall, or new circles invented **(187)**, it tells us that the writer hides himself or his most treasured thoughts for egocentric reasons.

The open **b** indicates credulity. When it is closed tightly it shows caution and business ability. Without a loop it shows the power of constructive thinking **(188)**.

When a small **c** has an initial stroke it reveals attention to detail. Keenness and mental development are indicated by the

189 ⟋ᴄ ᴄ ᴄ

angular **c**, and the round **c**, like all other rounded forms, indicates gentleness **(189)**.

190

Where the **d** has a loop it shows sensitiveness. The writer is rather susceptible to flattery. The **d** with a space between the last two strokes tells us that the writer is reticent. A long vertical stroke at the end of the **d** moving to the lower zone indicates obstinacy and a desire to control every situation. The Greek **d** is an expression of culture and often appears with the Greek **e** and the **g** made like a figure 8. The Greek **d** with the flourish indicates flirtatiousness. The low-stemmed **d** indicates shrewdness **(190)**.

191

When the Greek **e**, which indicates refinement, is accompanied by the Greek **d** and the **g** made like an 8, it usually indicates literary ability **(191)**.

The way in which we pen our **es** is far more varied than with any other small letter. Let us see some examples:

192

No final stroke **(192)**: prudent, reticent, rather selfish.

193

Short final stroke **(193)**: reticent, retiring.

194

Long final stroke **(194)**: generous, liberal.

G

195 Very long final stroke (195): extravagant.

196 Final stroke rising (196): self-conscious, living in clouds, impractical.

197 Final stroke curls over (197): protective, having desire to shield others.

198 Final stroke rises to right (198): brave, daring, willing to take a chance.

199 Final stroke curls under (199): self-centred, rather selfish.

200 Weak descent of final stroke to right (200): timid, weak-willed.

201 Strong descent to the right (201): obstinate, quick tempered.

202 Final stroke descends weakly, almost vertically (202): possessing strong likes and dislikes.

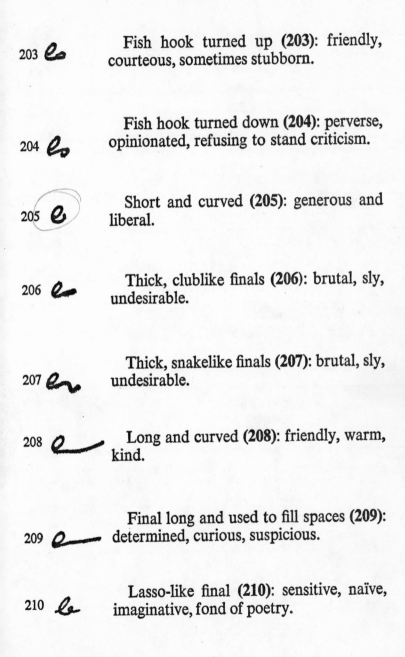

203 Fish hook turned up **(203)**: friendly, courteous, sometimes stubborn.

204 Fish hook turned down **(204)**: perverse, opinionated, refusing to stand criticism.

205 Short and curved **(205)**: generous and liberal.

206 Thick, clublike finals **(206)**: brutal, sly, undesirable.

207 Thick, snakelike finals **(207)**: brutal, sly, undesirable.

208 Long and curved **(208)**: friendly, warm, kind.

209 Final long and used to fill spaces **(209)**: determined, curious, suspicious.

210 Lasso-like final **(210)**: sensitive, naïve, imaginative, fond of poetry.

211   Final stroke turned down **(211)**: calm, matter-of-fact.

212   Final stroke like pigtail **(212)**: selfish.

213   Final stroke a flourish **(213)**: vain.

214   No loop **(214)**: keenness.

215   Greek **e** **(215)**: refinement.

216   Greek **e** with Greek **d** **(216)**: literary talent.

Now let us sum up in brief some small letters other than those with which we have dealt in this section.

217   Pointed top **(217)**: easily adaptable to circumstances.

218 *m* Rounded top **(218)**: not easily adaptable to circumstances.

219 *R* Small capital in middle of word **(219)**: affected.

220 *V N* Various styles of **r (220)** which betoken
r z quick, active mind.

221 *S* Printed small **s (221)**: talented, capable of constructive thinking (like other printed letter formations).

222 *J J w* Flying loop **(222)**: poetic, of simple nature.

The style of the small letters tells us important things about the writer. Are they angular, rounded or both? If you study the letters **m, n, v, w, x** you will see that many times a handwriting falls into both the angular and rounded categories. The bases of the letters are rounded and the tops are sharp and angular. We can deduce from this that the mind is keen whilst the nature is gentle. The writer is adaptable.

It is often a useful tip, when looking for arcades and angles, to turn the page upside down. The rounded or angular forms may then be spotted more easily.

Chapter 7

Horizontals and the *t* bar

GRAPHOLOGY assumes that the horizontal line in a script is an indication of the writer's plans for the future and with regard to his fellow men. That is when the horizontal bar has been written with a right-tending movement. The same horizontal bar written with a left-tending movement must reflect the writer's regression towards his past. Very few of us have no plans with respect to our future and our fellow men, so that the right-tending horizontal stroke can be found in almost everyone's script. The left-tending, more or less horizontal stroke has been found to be most typical of the poet, historian, musician and, of course, the egoist.

In the upper zone there are two prominent horizontal strokes—the small **t** bar and the stroke that covers the capital **T**. Short **t** bars appear in the script of timorous people who have little confidence in their own ideas and therefore do not plan very far ahead. The short **t** bar is also indicative of the sober and matter of fact. Those excessively long and fine **t** bars reveal the dreamer and the schemer. Planning too far ahead, he dreams of successes he is rarely able to achieve. He lacks common sense as well as a sense of proportion, and he may be a trifle lazy.

The horizontal strokes also indicate the balance in the character, and determine how much willpower and confidence the writer possesses. There are at least fifty

different kinds of **t** bars which have so far been discovered by graphological researchers, which seems to
indicate that human beings express strength and weakness in many ways. In this chapter I am giving examples
of those which appear most of all. Any other type you
see will probably be a variation of one of these.

There are only two kinds of horizontal stroke in the
lower zone—one with pressure and the other without.
We underline a word because we wish to draw the
reader's special attention to it. The horizontal stroke
underlining the writer's signature indicates an unconscious desire for importance, fame or greatness. The
habit of underlining words and phrases has always been
associated with people who insist on their own opinions,
whether or not they offend anyone. A horizontal stroke
in the lower zone, pressureless and short and not below
the writer's name, is indicative of the unconscious desire
to dominate. It is the prerogative of the feminine writer,
the domestic tyrant. It is the nagger's stroke. When it is
written with pressure we can count on it that the writer
is willing to fight anyone who dares to contradict him.

Now let us take a look at the main examples of **t** bars.

 Long and weak **(223)**: lacking self-
confidence.

 Short **(224)**: timorous, unable to change
ways and habits.

225 Cross to right **(225)**: lively, enthusiastic.

226 Cross to left (226): cautious, hesitant.

 227 Long and firm (227): prone to quick decisions, but not thorough, apt to rush things.

228 Long and to the right (228): impulsive and creative.

 229 Thin bar (229): weak-willed.

 230 Thick and firm bar (230): determined, self-assured.

231 Very low (231): kind, humble.

232 Very high (232): imaginative, irritable, prone to building castles in the air.

 233 No bar (233): careless, absent minded.

 234 Slanting up (234): desiring self-improvement.

235 Slanting down (235): obstinate, contrary.

236 Slanting decidedly down (236): critical about all except himself, stubborn, inclined to fight.

237 Down and curved (237): ability to mimic.

238 Up-turning hook at right (238): tenacious, perhaps greedy, envious.

239 Up-turning hook at left (239): matter of fact, dry.

240 Down-turning hook at right (240): matter of fact, dry, tenacious.

241 Sideways S-shaped bar (241): sarcastic, having good repartee, jovial, humorous, able to mimic.

242 Bar grows from thin to thick (242): having a temper which grows gradually.

243 Bar goes from thick to thin (243): having a sudden temper which dies just as quickly as it rises, sarcastic, quick-tongued.

244   Very heavy bar **(244)**: possessing decided opinions, self-assured.

245   Horsewhip shape to bar **(245)**: prone to practical joking.

246   Pennant bar **(246)**: egoistic, prone to showing off.

247   Star-shaped **(247)**: sensitive, unable to take criticism.

248   Excessively long and fine bar **(248)**: prone to be a dreamer or schemer, planning too far ahead, dreaming of successes he is rarely able to realise.

249   Very short bar **(249)**: extremely timorous.

250   Final incurve **(250)**: jealous, selfish, with no will of his own (may be controlled by will stronger than his own).

251   Clublike bar sloping down **(251)**: of uncertain temper, perhaps cruel.

252   Knotted **(252)**: persistent, with instinctive perseverance.

253 Angled **(253)**: sensitive, lacking initiative in situations where he might meet criticism.

254 Flying away to right **(254)**: animated, enthusiastic, impatient, perhaps possessing a hasty temper.

255 Type of pennant tied to left **(255)**: exactingly persistent, obstinate.

256 Downstroke reaches into lower zone **(256)**: opinionated, wilful.

257 Like an **o** with flying bar **(257)**: persistent about personal wishes.

258 Flying away above downstroke **(258)**: imaginative, with a tendency to reach for the unattainable, possessing a spirit of adventure.

259 To the left without touching downstroke **(259)**: apt to start things he does not finish.

260 Flying away to left **(260)**: neurotic, weak, aggressive.

261 Downstroke looped, **t** bar on left **(261)**: hypersensitive.

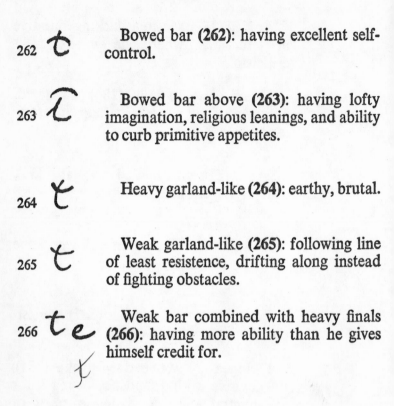

262 Bowed bar **(262)**: having excellent self-control.

263 Bowed bar above **(263)**: having lofty imagination, religious leanings, and ability to curb primitive appetites.

264 Heavy garland-like **(264)**: earthy, brutal.

265 Weak garland-like **(265)**: following line of least resistance, drifting along instead of fighting obstacles.

266 Weak bar combined with heavy finals **(266)**: having more ability than he gives himself credit for.

The i dot

Although **i** dots are usually taken in conjunction with other signs in handwriting—especially the type of **t** bar—there are a few with special significance. One is the circle **i** dot which shows that there is something different in the writer—perhaps a mild eccentricity. At any rate, the desire to be different is indicated in this type of dot, and the writer often resorts to attention-drawing devices such as manner of dress, speech which is not strictly conventional, or the kind of work he chooses. It is also an artistic sign and is often found in the handwriting of people who work in the field of art or design. What about the person who does not dot his is? You will find that he is absent-minded about what to him are unimportant details. But those i dots which do appear tell quite a few stories to the discerning eye. Let us take some samples now.

267 Close and directly above (267): precise, careful, with a retentive memory.

268 To the right (268): impulsive, intuitive, enthusiastic.

269 High to the right (269): curious, imaginative.

270 To the left (270): cautious, hesitant.

271 Directly above and very low (271): having good powers of concentration.

272 Very heavy (272): strong-willed, materialistic.

273 Light and weak (273): weak-willed, timid.

274 Circular **(274)**: self-conscious, egoistic, having a desire to be different and with artistic talent. *problems at home.*

 275 Like a dash **(275)**: vivacious, enthusiastic, irritable, worried.

276 Hooked or curved **(276)**: humorous, witty.

277 Shaped like a tent **(277)**: critical.

278 No dot **(278)**: careless, absent-minded.

Chapter 8

The final analysis

WITHOUT method there is chaos. This applies particularly to the science of handwriting analysis. A mixed up, haphazard system of analysis gives us a mixed up, haphazard picture of the writer. In order to achieve a clear, overall insight into the character and personality of the subject we must take, step by step, the various stages of analysis until the final picture emerges. Even then we must re-evaluate and re-assess until we are certain that we have not mistaken a tendency for a trait. We are taking a step towards a deeper knowledge of what goes to make the human mentality; we are learning something valuable which will stand us in good stead all our lives. We must take care to guard against mistakes.

Graphology is founded upon the science of psychology and psychoanalysis, and it is of great practical value in thousands of large business houses and employment agencies. It also leads to a better understanding of friends and acquaintances. Some of you may be a little puzzled by the many signs in handwriting which seem to have no commonsense connection with the character of the writer. What reasoning leads graphologists to conclude that the **g** made like a figure 8 indicates a taste for literature and adaptability? Or that those whose handwriting is very small are intellectually superior? What scientific basis is there for such conclusions? To be frank, we do not know completely. We only know that, from experience, the findings of graphologists have been statistically proved to be reliable, accurate and dependable.

When the graphologist labels certain signs with definite characteristics, he is merely making use of the results of hundreds of years of research, though he may not always know why the results occur. Unquestionably there are deep psychological reasons for the various characteristics in handwriting, but they are difficult to trace with certainty. What it really boils down to is that patient cataloguing and observation over centuries have taken graphology out of the guesswork stage and made it a truly deductive science.

Any science, any research must proceed step by step to the final conclusion. That is why I have endeavoured in this book to lead the layman methodically through each stage on to the next and the next until the final analysis. Individual graphologists have their own methods. I prefer to take the various analytical stages as follows:

1 Symmetry; 2 Pen pressure; 3 Margins; 4 Direction of lines; 5 Space between lines; 6 Space between words; 7 Space between letters; 8 Slant; 9 Size; 10 Garlands; 11 Arcades; 12 Angles; 13 Threads; 14 Concealing strokes; 15 Diagonal strokes; 16 Counter strokes; 17 Capitals; 18 Loops; 19 e finals; 20 other small letters; 21 The horizontal bar; 22 The t bar; 23 The i dot.

So on to the final analysis. Pictured here is part of a letter from a man aged forty-eight to a friend.

A quick glance or two and we see that certain characteristics are prominent. We note almost immediately the widening left margin which indicates haste, impatience, enthusiasm, oblivion to economic necessities and a certain innate lavishness. We see that the lines of and, of course, we shall be away in Europe for at least two months. We cannot pass the Quarantine regulations which means that Bonzo will not be coming with us.

Would it be too much to ask you to look after him whilst we are away? I feel sure he will not be too much trouble and, indeed, he should be company for you on the long evenings when Bill is away. Sarah would

---

writing slope upwards—sign of a pushing, buoyant spirit, ambition, optimism, restlessness. We observe the Greek **e** coupled with the Greek **d**, an indication of literary talent. But let us not move too swiftly towards a conclusion which may lack certain important elements. Let us take the analysis stage by stage.

Symmetry

The upper, middle and lower zones appear to be well-proportioned. Generally there is uniformity which indicates a certain even, peaceable temperament, a fondness for order, serenity or indifference or rigidity or callousness or apathy—other corroborating signs will tell us which. Re-examine the writing for symmetry. Is there, perhaps, a tendency towards an over-developed middle zone? There may be a sentimental or feminine streak in the writer's make-up. He may have an over-compensated inferiority complex, giving an impression of conceit. Other signs as we go on with the analysis will tell us if this is true.

Pen pressure

This is no fine script nor a heavy one. There is no pressure which makes the writing shaded. There are no smears. The pressure appears to be medium-heavy—which by itself tells us little.

Margins

Upper and lower margins neither wide nor narrow—a balance between the extrovert and the introvert. Right margin rather narrow, indicating vitality and the courage to face life, together with a certain haste. There is also the ability to be a good mixer. The left margin is interesting. Notice how it widens considerably towards the base of the letter. This will indicate to us haste, impatience, enthusiasm. The writer is innately lavish and oblivious to economic necessities. Probably his attempts at thrift often fail because of that innate lavishness.

Direction of lines

The lines are obviously ascending so we see that the writer possesses a pushing, buoyant spirit, ambition, optimism, restlessness. A few of the lines tend to be arched. Perhaps this indicates a tendency to have too little stamina in achieving an ambition. The writer may lose interest before his aim is reached. However, this is outweighed by the rest of the lines on the page. We might reach the conclusion that the writer will probably give up on the way to an ambition if the achieving of it means uninteresting or boring work— but will slog away to the final conclusion at work which really interests him.

Space between lines

We see that the spacing between the lines is a little wider than average—but not too much so. The writer possesses an analytical mind and the capabilities of a good organiser and executive. He has the capacity for clear presentation of complicated facts, is well-mannered, clean, reasonable, considerate.

Space between words

There appear to be sizeable, fairly even spaces between the words. Here we have the man who is interested in literature, who is fond of music and poetry, who may have deep feelings and firmly rooted convictions, who is at times cautious and rather critical, and who is an introvert. This latter characteristic clashes rather with our previous analysis of the right margin. But the upper and lower margins tell us that the subject is balanced between the extrovert and the introvert. We can, it seems, accept that—provided we get corroboration as the analysis proceeds.

Space between letters

Some of the letters are unconnected. The writer is obviously inventive, has initiative, is perhaps an ideas man. Again we have the critical characteristic. And the subject is an individual, self-reliant, artistic and intuitive in thinking and acting.

Slant
A definite right slant. Again we have optimism, together with spontaneity. Again we have initiative. We have strong sympathies and antipathies which go with the firmly rooted convictions indicated by his spacing between words. Courage, ambition, idealism together with a drive for independence. He is courageous, perhaps a little aggressive, with a pioneer spirit. Impetuous and affectionate, he is a humanitarian and an advocate of marriage in the prevailing sense.

The impetuosity indicated by his slant conflicts with the indications of caution in his word-spacing, but this impetuosity is corroborated to a certain extent by the haste and impatience indicated by his left margin. We might, in the final analysis, be forced to discount this pointer to caution.

Size
The script is a wide one. We assume imagination, warmth, artistic talent. Again initiative, spontaneity, courage, the inclination to be a good mixer. Perhaps he is rather boastful, given to fantasy, a little insincere— there may be corroboration later on.

Garlands
There is a slight tendency to enclosing garlands in the ws and in the y on line 15. They may amount to little— but there is that indication of a slightly scheming nature, narrow minded and perhaps at times practising calculated kindnesses together with mental reservation.

Arcades
There is no sign of those high arcades which point to poise, pride, a certain profundity. At the same time the occasional flat arcade is evident—which again may point to a slightly scheming nature, unobtrusive and perhaps a little hypocritical.

Angles
The angles are there joining the letters and, indeed, in the letters themselves. Note the **m**, the **n**, the **h**. Quick and firm, they indicate a certain reliability and imperturbability in working habits.

Threads
There is no sign of any real threads in the writing. But the S-link is there in the **y** and the capital **I**. We can assume that the writer will at times rely on his instinct and intuition for guidance. He may have ambitious aims which he pursues instinctively and blindly without regard for bourgeois considerations. He is probably good in negotiation and adaptable to any circumstance.

Concealing strokes
Definitely in the upper zone. Note the **h** in line 1, the **l** in line 5 and others. There is secrecy about the writer's plans and ideas.

Diagonal strokes
Not evident.

Counter strokes
Evident in the **ms** showing a slight amorality.

Capitals
The **B** is open at the base, indicating generosity. The **S** is a printed one, indicating constructive thinking.

Loops
There seems to be almost a habitual absence of loops in both the upper and the lower zones—many of the formations are concealing strokes, others are non-existent, which will indicate a certain uncluttered thinking. Note some of the **g**s and some of the **y**s—like numbers—and the **q**, too. They indicate good judgment and mathematical ability. The **f** has the return stroke to the left which tells us that the writer is quick in mind with fluent thought.

e Finals
The Greek **e** here coupled with the Greek **d**—which indicates literary talent.

Other small letters
The **a**s and **o**s stand out. They are fortified with a double wall and in some cases new circles are invented. The writer has the habit of hiding his feelings and his most treasured thoughts for egocentric reasons. The **m** and the **n** with the pointed top indicate an easy adaptability to circumstances which we also found in the S-link. The printed small **s** shows that the writer is talented and capable of constructive thinking.

The horizontal bar
Not evident in lower zone.

The t bar
Quite a variety here—which indicates adaptability and imagination. But predominant among them is the slightly weak, garland-like bar which tells us that the subject follows the line of least resistance. He drifts along instead of fighting obstacles and often takes the easiest way out. There is a suggestion in lines 3 and 8 that the writer is sensitive and may not like criticism.

In lines 4 and 6 there are suggestions that the writer makes quick decisions, is not thorough, and is apt to rush things.

The i dot
High and slightly to the right. The man is imaginative—and curious. But in lines 12 and 16 the **i** dot has been omitted, telling us of carelessness or absent-mindedness —or both.

Conclusion
There we have it. The personality of the man is laid bare, but it is slightly confused. Some of the characteristics—indeed most of them—are corroborative, but there are others in conflict. It is up to the analyst to assess and evaluate each trend or trait, then the clear picture will emerge. From the symmetry we see that the man has an even, peaceable temperament. He is subject to serenity despite his enthusiasm and impatience because the warmth indicated by the size of his writing cancels out indifference, rigidity and callousness. The enthusiasm indicated so often cancels out apathy.

The margins tell us that the writer is well-balanced, has vitality and the courage to face life, together with the ability to be a good mixer. They also tell us, as do other characteristics, that there is haste, impatience and enthusiasm, and an innate lavishness. The direction of the lines tell us of ambition and optimism as does the slant, but on the negative side the writing hints at a slight lack of stamina in working to achieve an ambition when that work may be tedious. The space between the lines indicates an analytical mind and good organising ability with good manners. The space between words indicates an interest in literature and music. Indeed, the Greek **e** with the Greek **d** points to literary ability. This word spacing and the siant both tell us of strong sympathies and antipathies. In both the letter-spacing and the size we see evidence of an artistic nature or talent.

This man is also a schemer. We see evidence of this in both the arcades and the garlands. At the same time the slant tells us that he is a humanitarian and an advocate of marriage in the prevailing sense. Perhaps, in this permissive age, his belief in the strong bonds of marriage might account for the narrow-mindedness indicated by the garlands. He is also a little boastful—indicated by the size—and he may be given to fantasy. But the angles tell us of reliability and imperturbable working habits. The imperturbable man does not worry unduly and the strength of his reliability might be tempered somewhat by the carelessness or absent-mindedness indicated by the missing i dots.

Secrecy about his plans and ideas and about his feelings and emotions is evident in the concealing strokes and the letters a and o. At the same time he is generous (the open-based capital B), and warm (the size). Easily adaptable to circumstances (the S-link and the m and n) he has good judgment, mathematical ability and a quick mind (the loops). The predominant t bar, however, tells us of a weakness which displays itself when he meets obstacles—he follows the line of least resistance and often takes the easiest way out.

Now let us tabulate his positive and his negative characteristics:

Positive
Even, peaceable temperament; fondness for order; serenity; good balance; vitality; courage; good mixing ability; ambition; optimism; analytical mind; good organising ability; good manners; cleanness; considerateness; fondness for music and poetry; literary talent; artistic ability; intuitiveness; self-reliance; inventiveness;

initiative; affection; humanitarianism; belief in marriage in the prevailing sense; imagination; warmth; imperturbability in working habits; adaptability; negotiating ability; generosity; constructive thought; uncluttered thought; good judgment; mathematical ability; quickness of mind.

Negative

Sentimentality; slight femininity (this could mean a softer, more sympathetic nature towards his fellow men or an aversion to killing, capital punishment, blood sports, etc); over-compensated inferiority complex; innate lavishness; lack of stamina in achieving an ambition; criticism; impetuosity; haste; impatience; boastfulness; insincerity; addiction to fantasy; narrow-mindedness; scheming nature; secrecy as regards plans and feelings; weakness in following the line of least resistance; sensitivity; lack of thoroughness; carelessness; absent-mindedness.

Chapter 9

The address on the envelope

AT first thought it would seem that not much can be learned from the written address on the envelope. We have been told that, in order to make a comprehensive analysis, we really need two full pages of handwriting, and here there are only four or five short lines at the most. But nothing is so distinctly governed by a purpose as the address on an envelope. In effect, it is an order to the Post Office to deliver the letter to that particular man or woman or firm whose name is written on the envelope. In order to enable the Post Office officials to read it easily, we must be clear and regular and stick to the conventions as laid down in the country in which we write it.

A writer who pens unintelligibly or who avoids the orthodox display shows that he puts his personal preferences or idiosyncracies before the demands of an ordinary and commonly-accepted purpose. He also displays a lack of consideration for others. But the motives of the person who writes unintelligibly will probably be entirely different from those of the person who avoids display by, say, writing too small. Emotional complexity or preoccupation with what is inside the letter may cause him to write unintelligibly—or he may avoid display because of a dislike of self-dramatisation. The two are connected in that both are unwilling to perform a public function the conventional

way, or accept a generally accepted common purpose.

Another interesting aspect of the written address is
the distribution of its parts on the envelope. The title
and name are usually placed slightly to the left, then
the house number and street starting a little to the right,
then the town—again a little to the right, then the
district or county or state—once more a little to the
right. The whole should be placed more or less in the
centre of the envelope area. Several divergent ways of
doing this have their own special significance.

An occupation of solely the left hand side of the

279

280

envelope **(279)** indicates a general clinging to security, the writer who will not take a chance, a readiness to run away from difficult situations. If the address occupies the upper part **(280)**, the writer is probably a dreamer, building castles in the air. Emphasis on the lower part **(281)** indicates a certain depression and materialism.

281
John Brake & Co Ltd
8, North John St,
Liverpool

282
Mr Brian Noon,
27, Cross Lane,
Bramhall,
Hants.

Placed in the centre **(282)**, the address reveals concentration, skill in putting ideas into practice, a certain conventionality. Generally on the right side **(283)**, the address indicates a more socially-minded man, one who

283

284

may put popularity first. Max Pulver sees in handwriting which develops like a ladder from the left edge of the envelope to the right **(284)** an indication of caution and distrust, of making contact little by little only.

Doodles

The drawings of nonsense pictures while one's attention is elsewhere have been described by one psychoanalyst as 'fugitives of the unconscious'. Doodles may be static constructions such as dots, geometrical figures or simple line patterns. Or they may contain animated forms such as animal shapes, grotesque living patterns or human faces. By themselves, they are difficult to decipher—one must take into consideration the associations which provide a clue to the emotional experiences underlying the slight evidence of the doodle. Without relevant data of the life history of the subject the riddle of the doodle may never be solved, for a doodle may symbolise some unconscious ambition held for years, some regression into a past pleasant or unpleasant experience.

There are, however, certain common symbols with a meaning so obvious that they can be interpreted without the help of the writer's associations. Among these symbols are squares and other geometrical forms which appear to indicate the ability to handle or deal with complexities. Triangles indicate the ability to rationalise; spider webs are connected to expanding associations; dots tell us of tension and concentration—they are also seen marking intersections in the doodles of persons who think precisely.

With the doodle, it appears that the adult is seeking unconscious release for certain of his emotions and repressions by reverting to the scribbling impulse of childhood. Children delight in scribbling; their random movements with a pen or pencil over the paper are the graphic equivalent of babbling, but unlike babbling, repetition indicates that the sequence of scribbling movements is performed in the child's own individual way. One child may use zigzag strokes, propelling the pencil with a tense and angular motion; another may use loose, circling movements that make whorls. In some children the movement may be restrained, in others sweeping and free. There may be forceful strokes; there may be only slight pressure.

Certainly the given pattern will be repeated again and again. It is the child's own, the conscious influenced by the unconscious, part of the pattern which will be evident in his writing when he becomes older. His scribbles are also indicative of his state of mind. Cheerfulness expands his line pattern; anxiety constricts it. Sadness reduces its size; aggressiveness shows in increased angularity; rage in an outburst of vehement strokes. In his scribbling the child creates and consistently uses his own individual movement pattern. When he is taught to write, however, he has temporarily to suppress his spontaneity and adapt himself to a rhythm and symmetry that are not his own. This means repression, and the thwarted urge seeks another avenue of release, probably in the underlining or adorning of letters and words that are emotionally meaningful to him. The habit of the child may well persist into adulthood. Signatures characterised by odd line elaborations seem strikingly to recall the scribbles of childhood, and even if these childish urges do not project into the ordinary handwriting, they may very well come out in the doodle.

It seems reasonable to regard doodles as projections of repressed emotions and thoughts, but the student of graphology must be warned that doodles have multi-determined meanings, and can be interpreted only in the light of associative content. The following are some of the more general and normal doodles from which the graphologist can gain certain clues to the thought pattern of the subject.

An arrow or arrows **(285)**: calculating, perhaps cruel temperamentally.

Separate square or squares **(286)**: tending towards the practical.

285–296 reading from left to right

Geometrically-linked squares **(287)**: having concrete practical skills.

Tightly drawn whorl **(288)**: tense, anxious.

Three-dimensional forms **(289)**: having a probing intellect.

Sharp, jagged lines **(290)**: undergoing a mood of resentment, even hostility (these doodles are often done during arguments).

Triangle **(291)**: having a strong, well-directed mind in adults. Exceptionally intelligent in children under six.

Flowing, curved figures **(292)**: easy going, good natured.

Circle **(293)**: 'closing up', warding off the outside world.

Steps and ladders **(294)**: having desire to climb up in the world.

Spider's web design **(295)**: preoccupied with self but seeking to widen horizons.

Random, helter-skelter figures without clear cut pattern **(296)**: prone to emotional conflict, confused in personality.

Tick marks **(297)**: concentrating on business in hand.

Frames **(298)**: having a feeling of fatalism, of being caught and frustrated by sex and life.

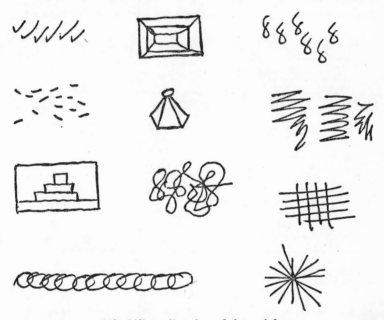

297–307 reading from left to right

Repetition **(299)**: able to enjoy his daily routine work.

Short confused dashes **(300)**: dynamic, colourful, forceful, creative, restless.

Three dimensional figure **(301)**: good at taking the easy way out.

Jagged lines **(302)**: aggressive, defensive.

Figure in a frame **(303)**: believing in safety first.

I

Involved design (304): shrewd, diplomatic, afraid of persecution.

Crossed bars (305): instinctively rebellious, pugnacious.

Linked circles (306): logical, inductive, consequential.

Spider's web without links (307): systematic, analytical, able to organise.

Chapter 10

Forgery

THE man in the street has only two sources of information on the methods by which the forging of handwritten documents is detected: prosaic and rather sketchy newspaper reports of law cases in fact, or the workings of the detective in fiction. In newspapers you read, perhaps, that the experts in a law case are directly at variance regarding the genuineness of a disputed document. Interest in the ingenious arguments for forgery changes to bewilderment as the other side begins using just as clever arguments for genuineness.

In the fictional detective yarns there are few such differences of opinion. The reader glimpses through other and more practised eyes things he could never see for himself. He watches the sleuth follow a clue to its logical conclusion in a manner bordering on the miraculous. The author must satisfy his reader by building up a situation that requires the bringing to light of obscure trifles that serve in the end as conclusive evidence. This is not all fantasy, of course. Many pieces of conclusive evidence in real life are those which escape the unpracticed eye of the layman.

The technology of graphology quite often does not enter into the detection of forgery. There are cases when a group of facts of a technical nature concerning the writing materials and not the writing itself is encountered. Take the case of an illuminated manuscript of a supposedly bygone age. The task is not to determine whether it was written by a certain person but whether it dates from the sixteenth century or not. On examining the ink we find that it is a type made no earlier than the nineteenth century. When we inspect the paper we get a similar result—so further proof becomes superfluous. But the paper may show evidence of being about four centuries old, and a writing fluid known to have been in use hundreds of years ago is evident of the manuscript. The parchment itself is worn and yellow with age, has an ancient appearance and soiled patches as if it has passed through many hands. Let us use a stereo-microscope on the manuscript. What do we see? The film of dirt lies under and not above the writing. The paper must have been soiled before the writer penned his illuminated script. Would he carry out his work on a soiled parchment? Here we could have proof that the so-called antique manuscript is artificial. This test applies equally to modern materials. It will enable us to tell whether a document has been falsified by additions, alterations or retouching.

Supposing a cheque was in dispute—perhaps the due-date or the amount has been declared false by one of the parties, though the signature is not in question. No graphologist will be able to tell whether someone did not change a 1 into a 9 by the addition of a small o without the help of some other scientific process. When a case of this kind is encountered, photography gives valuable aid. Enlarge the figure 9 under a powerful ray of light falling at a slant and we may see clearly the difference in the two parts.

Let us take the case of a cheque, the amount of which is in dispute. Another 0 has been added to the figures and the wording or part of it has perhaps been erased or altered. In this case it is important to discover whether the written word did not at some point come into contact with another part of the text. Microscopic examination should show us which of the crossed lines lies above the other. Should one word in the third line prove to have been written before the fourth line and another prove to have been written after, it should be evident that the amount has been altered. In the case of erasure of the original amount—by an eraser or by a liquid solvent—photographs taken with a quartz lamp should show the document as it appeared before being tampered with, for though the greater part of the ink adheres to the surface of the paper, a small amount will penetrate below the surface enough to show traces. Though the image may be somewhat blurred, a quartz lamp photograph will bring out that which is invisible to the naked eye.

In these cases the attention of the expert is directed not so much to an examination of the handwriting as to the mechanical and material conditions which prevailed during the act of writing. These are 'local forgeries' in contrast to forgeries of the entire text.

Now let us take a will which contains a codicil. The codicil, it is claimed, is not the work of the testator but has been added by forgery. An examination of the paper and of the ink is of no real value to the investigator, nor are there any other factors which might help. There is nothing for it but to call in the aid of the graphologist as only the evidence of the writing itself will be of use to establish the true authorship. We must make a comparison of the disputed document with the writing of the parties between whom the choice lies.

If you attempt to imitate somebody else's handwriting, the result will turn out to be less a written than a drawn copy. Fluent or rapid motion is impossible in copying. The tempo is always slow and even the most practised forger is in the end subject to a falling off in concentration. He will interrupt his work more frequently than anyone writing naturally, and laboured writing means uncertainty—evident in trembling and interrupted strokes. Again, a forger is not likely to be satisfied with first results—he will touch up his work here and there. And as this retouching occurs he will change his grip on the pen, holding it, perhaps, at varying angles to the paper.

These are the primary symptoms, evidenced by slow writing; uncertain, slightly broken or trembling strokes; letters which have been gone over again; changes in the

It was a beautiful day. The sun was streaming down through the recently opened beech leaves. Dainty bluebells strained their head towards the sun.

In the nearby field a tiny brown mouse scurried for the shelter of a mouldering hay bale as I approached.

My dog barked impatiently when I paused to empty a stone from my boot. She cocked her head on one side as much as to say: "Get a move on, we haven't got all day.

Last weekend I went up to
London to visit friends. It
was the first time I had been
to the city for ages so I
took the opportunity of seeing
some of the famous sights.
Buckingham Palace was
first on the list, and we
enjoyed a cup of tea and
a couple of sandwiches
in St James's Park. Later
we went to the Victoria

grasp of the pen during writing. These primary symptoms are in many cases sufficient to satisfy the investigator, but for certainty the graphologist relies also on a character or personality reading of the two specimens.

There are two letters printed here. One of them is genuine; the other is a forgery. How do we tell this? The two are apparently written by the same person, but upon examination we find quite a number of graphological differences, some fairly obvious, some rather obscure.

We see from the **t** bars that the writter of letter No 1 has a rather quick temper which dies almost as suddenly as it arises. But examine the **t** bars in letter No 2. Here we have just the opposite. The bars grow from thin to thick, denoting a temper which grows gradually. And whereas the bars in letter No 1 slant upwards in the main, showing a desire for self-improvement, in letter No 2 most of them slant down, indicating obstinacy and contrariness. Indeed some of them slope decidedly down, giving the impression that the writer is critical about all except himself. There is stubbornness indicated in these bars too—but where is the corroborative evidence of that trait? There are certainly no abruptly-finished end strokes. We can safely say that the **t** bars in letter No 1 were not written by the writer of letter No 2.

The writer of letter No 1 is well able to keep a secret. We know that from the formation of the **o**s and **a**s. They are rather tightly closed at the top—indeed in many cases they are knotted, which indicates a really secretive nature. Now examine the **a**s and **o**s in letter No 2. They are well open at the top, indicative of a frank, open nature to whom secrecy is anathema. It appears that the true personality of letter No 2 writer has broken through his concentration on forgery—or perhaps he considers the formation of the **a**s and **o**s of little consequence in the overall picture.

The **i** dots in letter No 1 are interesting. Some of them are to the right; some of them high to the right; some of them directly above. From them we deduce that the writer is impulsive, enthusiastic, intuitive—and has a retentive memory (based upon the directly-above dot). The high dots indicate curiosity and imagination. But at no time are the dots markedly to the left. This is in direct contradiction to the dots in letter No 2 where we discover that all the **i** dots are situated on the left of the relative letter. Caution and hesitation indicated by these left-side dots cannot possibly be in harmony with the impulsive, enthusiastic, intuitive personality of the writer of letter No 1.

Let us take the margins. The left margin in letter No 1 is evenly wide. Here we deduce traits of self-respect, generosity, a good cultural background, perhaps a little reserve or shyness. The same traits are indicated in letter No 2—but only so far. Halfway through the letter the true personality of the writer begins to show through. He has lost a large amount of his concentration and we find the margin widening considerably. Haste, impatience, an oblivion to economic necessities are coming to the fore, and we find that this writer's attempts at thrift will fail as his innate lavishness breaks through. Whereas the margin on the right in letter No 1 is fairly even, that in letter No 2 appears decidedly irregular. There is an unsureness here, a lack of a sense of economy, an unwise thrift which appears to agree to some extent with the traits shown by the widening left margin. It seems the forger cannot prevent his true personality showing at times despite concentration.

Notice how, in letter No 1, the writer keeps more or less to the same horizontal level in the line-slope, indicating a certain composure and love of method. In letter No 2 we find the direction of the lines changes irregularly—an obvious pointer to unsteady working habits which is just the opposite to the trait shown in the first letter. Then again, the spacing between lines, whilst regularly wide in letter No 1, is decidedly confused in letter No 2—indicating a certain confusion in the writer's personality. Whilst taking some care in the formation of the individual letters, the forger has had insufficient knowledge of the science of graphology, and has made the mistake of ignoring the direction of the lines, the spacing between lines and the margins.

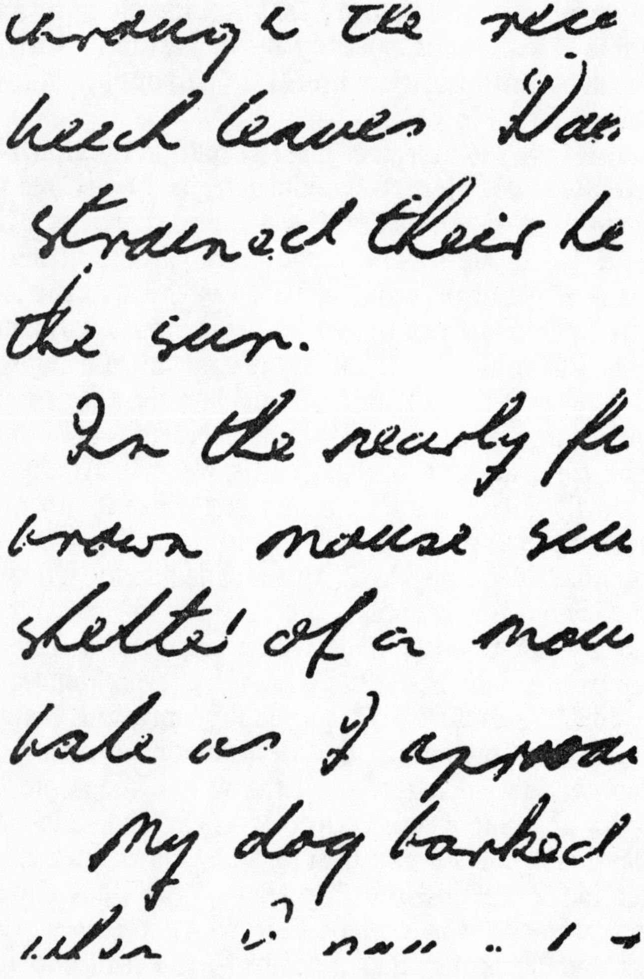
through the rece
beech leaves Wa
streamed their be
the sun.
In the nearly fu
brown mouse see
shelter of a mou
hole as I approa
My dog barked

Even without the aid of a graphological interpretation, letter No 2 suggests an obvious forgery. Examine the two photographic enlargements of portions of the letters, and even the most cursory eye will observe the laboured, trembling strokes as opposed to the clean sweeps of letter No 1. The clean lines of unconscious calligraphy in letter No 1 are replaced in letter No 2 by the shaky lines which denote concentrated care. There is also a bit of touching up to be noticed.

We have, up to now, been comparing two different letters at the same time. One method which many noted examiners of questioned documents adopt is that which takes each note entirely separately for analysis—then compares the two finished analyses.

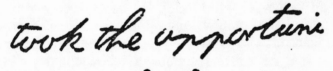

Chapter 11

The history of graphology

JUDGED by ordinary standards the science of graphology is young, and it is in only the last half century that it has reached any true psychological depth. The field is still wide open to research, both on the physical and psychological planes. It is only recently that graphology has left behind the status of an intuitive art and become a practical science. The first specialised book dealing with the relationship between handwriting and the writer's character and personality was published in 1622 by an Italian, Camillo Baldi. He was a doctor of medicine and philosophy and Professor of Theoretical Medicine at the University of Bologna. At the same time that he wrote his book a fellow-countryman, a professor of anatomy named Marcus Aurelius Severinus, was engaged upon a similar work, but before he could publish it he died in 1656 from the plague.

The number of treatises and articles cn the subject increased considerably from the mid-seventeenth century throughout Europe. In the eighteenth century came really important studies from the Swiss physiognomist Georg Lavater, and in 1812 the French writer Louis Hocquart published anonymously a collection of studies in book form. It was in France that the real origins of modern graphology were founded. Members of the higher French clergy in the early nineteenth century formed a study circle which systematically examined the relationship between human qualities and their graphic expression in handwriting. Among this group were Cardinal Regnier, Archbishop of Cambrai, Bishop Boudinet of Amiens and the Abbé Flandrin. It was Flandrin who became the teacher of the man acknowledged to be the founder of modern scientific graphology, Jean Hippolyte Michon.

Michon was born in 1806 and died seventy-five years later after he had formulated almost all the signs and rules upon which graphology is still based. It was he, too, who established the name Graphology—from the Greek words grapho (I write) and logos (theory or doctrine). The Abbé Michon was a man of wide knowledge and many spheres of interest. Apart from books on many topics, he also published a number of novels, but he won his greatest success and permanent fame with graphology which he called an art and with which he worked only by experience and observation. During years of study he compared the handwriting of people with whose character he was familiar and, using his intuitive genius and great faculties of observation, he discovered the graphic signs which writers with similar deficiencies or qualities have in common.

Debarolle and Delèstre, two of his collaborators, heped him collect the signs of many human qualities, and from 1872 onwards he started producing an invaluable catalogue of graphological signs and rules based on his own experience. He did no theorising, however, and did not attempt to explain the probable reason for the production of these signs. Nor did he attempt to connect the psychology of handwriting with other branches of physiology or psychology. Michon was the forerunner of a French school later led by a pupil of his, Jules Crépieu-Jamin, which continued to emphasise experience and empirical comparison in their research. But Crépieu-Jamin later abandoned Michon's doctrine of definite signs which pointed to only one meaning, and evolved a more subtle system of co-ordination of dominant signs.

Later a scholar named Jules Depoin, who also edited a periodical, started a society for the study of grapho-logy, creating a centre for the research and discussion of the subject which drew into its midst prominent men such as Director of the Sorbonne Dr Binet, the sociolo-gist G. Tarde, and Arsène Aruss. Meanwhile, in Germany, Adolf Hentze was working as a graphological practitioner for a periodical in Leipzig and captivating readers of the journal with a series of fascinatingly correct handwriting analyses. His series drew the atten-tion of many scholars to the subject, but his books and articles did little to aid the development of research.

In Austria in the 1850s a professor of economics, E. Schwiedland, published articles and a book based on the discoveries of the French school, but economics was his main bent and gradually absorbed all his attention to the exclusion of graphology. He had, however, left a legacy in the shape of gifted pupils, among whom was the German Wilhelm Langenbruch. With the Austrian woman scholar named Rudolphine Poppee and a few others he worked on so that the new science should be recognised. In 1895 he founded a periodical, *Deutsche Graphologische Gesellschaft,* devoted entirely to graphology, then introduced two doctors of medicine to assist his researches. One of them, Dr William Preyer, a university professor of medical physiology, was born in England, went as a child to Germany and later founded the new theory which took into account the physiology, psychology and pathology of handwriting and so con-nected graphology with the other achievements of modern science.

Hans Busse in 1897 founded a society for grapho-logical research and a second periodical, *Graphologische*

Monatshefte, in Germany. A gifted practitioner and able organiser, he had edited a German edition of Crépieu-Jamin's main works, and for this new periodical he enlisted as contributors Dr Georg Meyer, a psychiatrist to a German mental home, and Dr Ludwig Klages, the most important research worker and the acknowledged high priest of the German theoretical school. Dr Meyer published a book in which he systematically analysed the scientific and theoretical basis of handwriting psychology, in particular the spontaneity of writing impulses.

Ludwig Klages took the limelight by writing many books on the problems of philosophy and the psychology of expression. He was also the first to create and complete a systematic theory of graphology and to see in handwriting the expression of the human personality as a whole, fitted into its place with the other doctrines of human expression and character. His system clearly defined the various meanings of every single handwriting trend according to a general law of polarity—that is, the same trend can denote one quality in one handwriting and the converse of the same quality in another. His researches were based on a conception of writing as a conflict between natural impulses and rhythms on the one hand and mental discipline on the other. His new system of analysis was based on a general standard of handwriting. To him the standard of writing was high when the writer succeeded in reconciling his genuine personal rhythm with the requirements of disciplined writing. The standard was lower by the degree to which the writer failed to achieve this reconciliation.

By analysing the changeable and unchangeable elements in handwriting, he found a way to reveal both intentional and unintentional disguise. But Klages' system had its deficiencies. He over-emphasised his personality conception, and his rather rigid plan of compressing human nature on standards of value based on his ideals of personality does not allow for the relativity of all tendencies in human character.

Robert Saudek, who came from Czechoslovakia and finished his main works in England earlier this century, explored the connection between graphology and the psychology of the unconscious. He was especially concerned with the differences between national characters and national copybook writing. He made a special study of English writing, with the accent on research into that most important factor—speed.

Max Pulver, the Swiss, partially abandoned Klages' abstract and idealistic conception of personality and linked graphology with the discoveries of the psychology of the unconscious. He emphasised the strong symbolic element in handwriting, and especially illuminated the problem of what the writing space symbolises in the writer's mind. He studied extensively the writings of criminals, as did the Italian psychiatrist Professor Lombroso, the Austrian Dr Wieser and many others.

The graphological characteristics of illnesses have been dealt with in many books, and research into the physiological aspects of handwriting analysis culminated in a book by Duparchy in which he attempted a general diagnosis of all illnesses—but the attempt proved unsatisfactory. More research is needed—much more.

However, Lombroso, the Austrian psychiatrist Pick, the German Koster, the Frenchman Dr Rogues de Fursac and many others have made valuable studies of the writings of patients suffering from mental and nervous diseases. Many great English writers and artists have been attracted by handwriting over the centuries— Scott, Poe, the Brownings, Byron, Disraeli, the painter Gainsborough among them. The first Englishman to deal with the relation between character and handwriting to any great extent was Stephen Collett, who published a book on the subject in 1823. The Continental graphology was introduced to England and popularised by Shooling, who translated the main works of Crépieu-Jamin. Later, Robert Saudek, the handwriting expert from Prague, brought the German theoretical school to England. One of his pupils, C. H. Brooks, wrote a textbook based on Saudek's system which was later translated into German. In 1936 another prominent Continental graphologist, H. J. Jacoby, arrived in England and published some books there.

Meanwhile, the study of graphology had become popular in the United States, and was there to become a potent factor in the armoury of personnel selection consultants, psychiatry experts and insurance investigators as well as most branches of industry. Nadya Olyanova published a book on the subject of the psychology of handwriting. Klara G. Roman furthered investigations into the connection between personality and writing with a number of books. While in some parts of Europe graphology had reached university status, in America it had also ceased to be a parlour game and had become a clinical tool.

There are still great strides to be taken in psychiatry and medicine, and now it is recognised that many mental, emotional and physical diseases can be diagnosed with the help of graphology. There have been protests, particularly in America, at this so-called underhand method of personality and character reading, but more and more personnel managers in industry are applying it to their task of selection, particularly in the executive sphere.

K

Chapter 12

Scraping the surface

PROFESSOR H. J. RUPERT, one of the American school of lecturers in psychology who value a knowledge of graphology, uses a novel method of gaining a rather sketchy picture of the personality and character of his students. He asks each of them to draw a tree, and from the finished sketch he draws conclusions which, although they do not dig very deeply, have proved startlingly accurate. In his analysis he divides the tree into two parts—the trunk and the crown. Here are his conclusions:

TRUNK

Broad (a): exaggerated self-confidence.

Long and thin (b): self-confidence, pride, enthusiasm, Probable need for inner fulfilment. Intellectual ambitions.

Scars on trunk (c): still consciously or unconsciously plagued by an unfortunate experience.

Bends to the right (d): positive attitude towards life; enterprising; feels urge for activity; always ready to help.

Bends to the left (e): introverted; self-engrossed; may be dreamer.

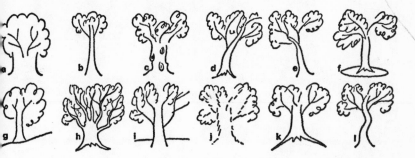

Set on island or hill-like line **(f)**: feeling of isolation or loneliness; reserved; independent.

Set on slanted ground line **(g)**: mistrustful; has some difficulty in adjusting; anxious.

Realistic, flaring trunk **(h)**: active; gifted; social; good sense of humour.

Ground line above bottom of trunk **(i)**: passive; shrinks from reality; longs for unobtainable.

Trunk drawn with short, separate lines **(j)**: impulsive; excitable; emotional; impatient.

Trunk flares into roots **(k)**: observant; secure; realistic; not easily upset by events.

Trunk makes several curves like moderate 'S' **(l)**: artistic; sensitive; may easily be hurt.

CROWN

Falls around trunk like sack **(m)**: indecisive; non-aggressive; subject to moods; easily led.

Fluffy cloud style **(n)**: imaginative; adjustable; companionable; sometimes conceited.

Circles within circles **(o)**: strong-willed; inflexible; egocentric; sometimes unresponsive.

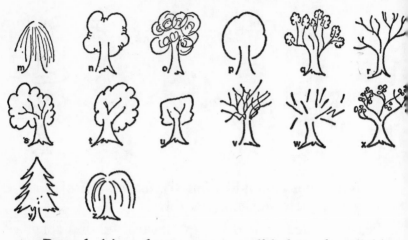

Round (p): calm; mature; well-balanced; reliable; honest.

Several cloud-like balls on several branches (q): diplomatic; pleasant; obliging; hides real reasons and motives.

Few leaves, bleak as winter tree (r): defensive; impatient.

Left side of crown larger or heavier (s): cautious; thoughtful; likely to fuss over small matters.

Right side of crown larger or heavier (t): adventurous; restless; may lack ability to concentrate; self-confident.

Flat, box-like crown (u): feels pressures; dependent; submissive.

Composed of confused lines (v): unmethodical; unconventional; acts on spur of moment; changeable.

Composed of uncoordinated lines (w): playful; sometimes thoughtless; impulsive; easily distracted; may lack self-control.

Has fruit (x): maturity; gift of self-dramatisation. Falling fruit may indicate feeling of loss or self-sacrifice.

Christmas tree shape (y): definite; orderly; strong-willed; may be bitter or sarcastic.

Long, drooping branches and crown like willow (z): feeling of defeat; withdrawal from world.

Bibliography

Baldi, Camillo. *Trattaro come da una lettera missiva si conoscono la natura e qualita del scrittore* (Bologna 1664)

Becker, Minna. *Graphologie der Kinderschrift* (Heidelberg 1926)

Biro, Jozsef. *A Modern Grafologia (Modern Graphology)* (Budapest 1930)

Brooks, C. H. *Your Character From Your Handwriting* (1946)

Busse, Hans H. *Die Handschriftendeutungskunde* (Munich 1896)

Crepieu-Jamin, J. *L'Ecriture et le Caractere* (Paris 1888)

— — *Les elements de l'ecriture des canailles* (Paris 1924)

Downey, June E. *Graphology and the Psychology of Handwriting* (Baltimore 1919)

Duparchy-Jeannez, M. *Les maladies d'apres l'ecriture* (Paris 1919)

Eng, Helga. *The Psychology of Children's Drawings* (New York 1931)

Gernat, Alfred. *Graphologische Praxis* (Villach 1948)

Heiss, Robert. *Die Deutung der Handschrift* (Hamburg 1943)

Jacoby, Hans. *Analysis of Handwriting* (New York 1940)

— — *Handschrift und Sexualitat* (Berlin 1932)

Klages, Ludwig. *Handschrift und Charakter* (Leipzig 1940)

Lessing, Theodor. *Charakterologie* (Halle 1926)

Lewinson, Thea, and Zubin, Joseph. *Handwriting Analysis* (New York 1942)

Lombroso, C. *Handbuch der Graphologie* (Leipzig 1902)

Mendel, A. O. *Personality in Handwriting* (New York 1947)

Meyer, G. *Wissenschaftliche Grundlagen der Graphologie* (Jena 1925)

Morf, G. *Praktische Charakterkunde* (Bern 1945)

Myer, O. N. *The Language of Handwriting* (1958)

Michon, J. H. *Les Mysteres de l'ecriture* (Paris 1872)

— — *La Methode pratique de Graphologie* (Paris 1878)

Osborne, Albert S. *Questioned Documents* (New York 1929)

Pulver, Max. *Symbolik der Handschrift* (Zurich 1945)

Rand, A. *Graphology* (1962)

Roman, Klara G. *Handwriting: A Key To Personality* (1954)
Saudek, R. *The Psychology of Handwriting* (1928)
—— *Experiments with Handwriting* (New York 1929)
Schneidemuehl, G. *Handschrift und Charakter* (Leipzig 1911)
Singer, Eric. *The Graphologist's Alphabet* (1950)
Sonnemann, Ulrich. *Handwriting Analysis* (New York 1950)
Wolfson, Rose. *A Study in Handwriting Analysis* (New York 1949)

Index